HIDDEN TREASURES

GLOUCESTERSHIRE

Edited by Simon Harwin

First published in Great Britain in 2002 by
YOUNG WRITERS
Remus House,
Coltsfoot Drive,
Peterborough, PE2 9JX
Telephone (01733) 890066

HB ISBN 0 75433 867 3
SB ISBN 0 75433 866 5

FOREWORD

This year, the Young Writers' Hidden Treasures competition proudly presents a showcase of the best poetic talent from over 72,000 up-and-coming writers nationwide.

Young Writers was established in 1991 and we are still successful, even in today's technologically-led world, in promoting and encouraging the reading and writing of poetry.

The thought, effort, imagination and hard work put into each poem impressed us all, and once again, the task of selecting poems was a difficult one, but nevertheless, an enjoyable experience.

We hope you are as pleased as we are with the final selection and that you and your family continue to be entertained with *Hidden Treasures Gloucestershire* for many years to come.

CONTENTS

English Bicknor CE Primary School

Samantha Oakley & Naomi Robbins	41
Sarah Bland	41
Merlin Rowles	41
Robyn Hunter	42
William Osborne	42
Joshua Evans	42
Miriam Hamilton	43
Timothy Greenman	43
Jessica Hone	43
Lucy Rowles	44
Matthew Lacey	44
Stephen Brown	44
Martyn Blakemore	45

Fairford CE Primary School

Jay Delves	45
Letty Indge	46
Katie Correia	46
Luke Martin	47
Alice Edwards	47
Becky Mumford	48
Harriet-Jade Harrow	48
Susie Taylor	49
Rachael Burton	50
Luke Maunder	50
Helen Gordon	51
Robin Taylor	51
Emma Yells	52
Robert Coggins	52
Hannah Embleton-Smith	53
Gemma Clarke	53
Holly Parker	54
Georgia Alice Hastings	55

Hardwicke Parochial Primary School

Sian Parnell	55
Amy Williams	56

Jessica Hynes	56
Ethan Wilkinson	57
Mary Edwards	58
Joe Alderman	58
Jasmine Dalmeny	59
Ross Howell	59
Ian Hawksworth	60
Rebecca Bamford	60
Harriet Higgins	61
Stacey Morgan	61
Jordan Rouse	62
Kelly Marie Fryer	63
Emily Mar-Gerrison	64
Samuel Jellyman	64
Cara-Leigh Taylor	65
Emma Higgins	66
Adam Cox	67
Daniel Sutton	67
James Parry	68
Becky Chapman	68
Kiya Marshall	69
Daniel Griffin	70
Laughna Morris	70
Chelsea Jones	71

Hopelands School

Lily Witchell	71
Chanelle Jones	72
Sophie McDonald	72
Phoebe Rodgers	73
Alexandra Radcliffe	74
Megan Smyth	74
George Perrins	75

Horsley CE Primary School

Esther Gooch	75
Harry Tate	76
James Ashton	76

Bertie Barr	77
Sophie Forster	77
Alfie Godden	78
Ellie Roberts	78
Charlotte Lee	79
Sophie Louisa Craven	79
Kieran Colvin	80
Rachel Savage	80
Lindsay Allen-Hynd	81
Rosie Jade Jenkins	81
Kelly Wright	82
Hannah Fullard	82
Oliver Huggett-Wilde	83
Charlotte Oatley	83
Emma Dean	84
Amber LeGay	84
Molly Wright	85
Kathryn Savage	85

Ingleside School

Bryony Smith	86
James Hale	86
Amelia Wreford	87
Emily Blampied	87
Madeleine Turner	87

Kingswood Primary School

Laura Kate Mansbridge	88
Lauren Aldridge	89
Catherine Scothern	90

Lakeside Primary School

Melissa Martin-Hughes	90
Becky Waterhouse	91
Annie Dickinson	92
Amy Higgins	92
Elliot Miller	93

Vanessa Cotton-Betteridge	94
Georgina Pugh	94

Mitton Manor Primary School

Cameron Harpin	95
Robert Jeal	96
Alex Williams	96
James Blencowe	97
Natalie Potter	97
Andrew Mobey	98
Tom Moss	98
Lauren Castello	99
Chloe Mason	99
Bethan Healy	100
Victor Andrew Howard	100
Jennifer Cromwell	101
Emma Paulson	101
Harry Foster	102
Emma Williams	102
Samantha Danter	102
Christopher Williams	103
Leanne Spry	103
Katie Cadwallader	104
Lizzie Clarke	105
Georgina Day	105
Oliver Francis	105
Thomas Allcoat	106
Owen Vincent	106
Annie Wilkinson	107
Laura Griffin	107
Sam Gray	108
Connor White	108

North Cerney CE Primary School

Joe Johnson	109

St David's Primary School, Moreton-In-Marsh

Kitty Mounstephen	109
Elizabeth Allen	110
Joe Ladbrook	110
Sade Peach	110
Carl Luker	111
Stephanie Ward	111
Daisy Perry	112
Sophie Wise	112
Samantha Jeffrey	113
Melissa Day	113
Megan Hartnell	114

St Lawrence Primary School, Lechlade

Nikolas Powis	114
Catherine Hope	115
Jenna Kennedy	116
Polly New	116
Alastair Blower	117
Katherine Dipple	118
Emma-Louise Pritchard	118
Victoria Button	119
Christina Codling	120
Alexandre Duncan	120
Jessica Martin	121
Isabella Richards	122
Christina Shields	122
Harriet Thomas	123
Chesney Gandhi	124
Chloë Nicoll	124
Ruth Howlett	125
Tom Traas	126
Katy Brewer	126
Lucinda Popp	127
Tia Gammond	128
Jack Marston	128
Stephanie Dyos	129

The Poems

HIDDEN TREASURE

Diving into the deep
My aqualung on my back
A string of pearls beside me
Those pearls are my breath
I'm like a shark
Cutting through the water
A fish swimming

I swim on past coral reefs and rocks
The rocks are like mountains
Coral reefs burst into fish
I see something shining ahead
I go to investigate
It is hidden treasure
Giant pearl necklace
Gold, silver and bronze coins

Lie about and right in the centre
There is a golden crown
I turn to swim back
To the surface
I take nothing with me.

Miranda Filmer (9)
Beaudesert Park School

THE AIRING CUPBOARD

In the warm airing cupboard,
Gorgeous smells wash out,
Reminding me of summery days.
Ironed, cleaned, folded and flattened,
The clothes are stacked like pancakes,
On the boring, smooth and plain shelves.

Amilia Buchan (9)
Beaudesert Park School

HIDDEN TREASURE

Planted and watered,
It will slowly send shoots up,
Forcing itself to the surface,
It grows into a colourful flower,
With a strong stalk and precious petals,
Under the ground where the worms wiggle,
It will grow,
From a tear,
The seed is a hidden treasure.

James Hillman (9)
Beaudesert Park School

SEASHELL

Along the golden, sandy beach,
Into the sparkling, sapphire sea,
A seashell lies in the darkness.
Inside its twirling, endless maze,
Smooth pale walls of a hollow cave.
Spikes lie across the cream-coloured,
Helpless surface of the spiralling shell.
It is the only precious jewel in the sandy beds.

Robin Silvey (9)
Beaudesert Park School

THE OYSTER

In the depths of the sea lies an oyster,
Outside bits of seaweed float towards him.
His shell is a crust of barnacled craters,
Inside a carpet of slithering slime.

Buried in his disgusting salty soup,
A circular shiny ball of snow.
This is the pearl, all silvery white,
Like the moon on a hot summer's night.

Alexander Warner (10)
Beaudesert Park School

DRAIN

Inside, a drip of unpleasant slime,
Echoes around the hollow chamber.
A whoosh of air flits past the scuttling rats.
Above the uncanny noise of the working world.
Nearby, is a pile of leaves,
It would be nothing,
But for a
Treasure from a lady's finger,
Underneath this pile of dirt.

Thomas Morley (9)
Beaudesert Park School

MY POCKET

Lurking in the shadows of my pockets,
Lies . . . old conkers going rotten,
A precious stone long forgotten.
A notepad with nothing in,
Old tissues destined for the bin.
Sweet wrappers smelling of honey,
Two pounds of jangling money.
The riches of a schoolboy's days.

James Priest (9)
Beaudesert Park School

THE LAUNDRY BASKET

Here is the laundry basket,
Dull and grey,
Under the lid,
A sunny day.
Dad's muddy trousers,
Mixed with Granny's skirt,
Concealed in it all,
Mum's gardening shirt.
Several coloured and exotic loads,
A tropical rainforest of clothes,
Infested with dirt and washing codes.
This is the laundry basket,
Dull and grey.

Freddie Miles (9)
Beaudesert Park School

HIDDEN TREASURE

On the paper, X marks the spot,
Where the hidden treasure was left and lost,
I followed the map to the top of the mountain,
Where I found a pretty fountain.

I dug and dug till I found,
A treasure box tall and round,
I opened the box and then I saw,
A thousand gold pennies and more

And still there was one more thing,
A pretty platinum, emerald ring.

Katherine Lindemann (10)
Beaudesert Park School

MY MOTHER'S HANDBAG

Inside my mother's handbag sits an ancient purse,
Blue with wrinkles like an old lady's face and hands.
Lipstick, glossy and rich with the colour of a midsummer sunset.
Loose change glimmers in the faintly-lit depths of this cavernous tomb.
A perfume bottle half-filled with a golden liquid shimmers.
A chequebook as black as panda's fur with pages the colour
                                         of candyfloss.
A pack of tissues with lavender scent.
A hairbrush often used, with prongs like a hedgehog's back,
Reflections of my mother's day.

Rachel Sykes (10)
Beaudesert Park School

TRAMP

Your filthy forehead is a whale,
The aged wrinkles compact.

Your eyes are of ice,
They stare into nothingness.

Your dry lips are chapped
And their colour is lost.

Your arms are bruised,
Each mark is a sorrow.

But somewhere inside lies a treasure,
That hidden prize is a golden heart.

Camilla Wade (10)
Beaudesert Park School

STABLE

Concealed inside the smelly stable, a horse,
With dust from hay and straw,
Lurking in buckets, food and water,
A salt lick hangs like a bunch of grapes,
You hear the crunching of teeth,
A juicy carrot nibbled from your hand,
A violet head collar slipped onto its head,
To lead it to the summer light.

Harriet Dembrey (9)
Beaudesert Park School

OYSTER

Barnacle-covered, shaped like a rock.
Rough like bark, grey as a mouse,
Deep in the sea an oyster's house.
Lying inside, a whirlpool of heaven,
Twirling and swirling, a glistening gem.
Right in the hub of a great glob of goo,
Which conceals the pearl hiding from you!

Thomas Dauncey (9)
Beaudesert Park School

TREASURES OF A TREE

Concealed inside the tree, rings like a maze,
Within the maze, a golden sticky sap like glue.
Below the tree a crunchy, crispy sound,
As orange autumn leaves burn with fire.

Down in the earth my roots burrow like moles,
Ants crawl up my trunk, while a perched robin sings,
I hear a roaring engine,
A huge monster lumbers towards me - tree cutters.

Sam Browne (9)
Beaudesert Park School

MY MOTHER'S HANDBAG

Outside you are a smooth plate,
Inside you are a small dark tunnel,
Buried in the gloom is a notebook,
A large and clumsy purse,
An apple, small and juicy,
A bunch of keys, cold and shiny,
A pen to scribble shopping lists,
Each little object shows what a busy life the handbag holds.

Annabel Ricketts (10)
Beaudesert Park School

SEA

In the deep blue,
Lies an oyster.
Outside a pimpled shell,
Disguises the tomb,
Concealing a secret,
In the sandy slimy goo.
A pearl like the moon,
Locked behind a hinged door.

William Warner (9)
Beaudesert Park School

POCKETS

Lurking in my pockets,
A mouldy crumbling biscuit,
Coated in soft grey fluff.

Buried in the shadows,
A smooth shiny conker,
Tied to its string.

Concealed by the dark,
A thick rectangular book,
Connected to a blunt red pencil.

Obscured by the gloom,
A silver twenty pence piece,
Promise of sugary treats.

That's what hides in my pockets,
Dull and murky as the grey sky.

Freddie Gardner (9)
Beaudesert Park School

INSIDE THE SHIP

Inside the ship a dreary day,
In and out of portholes fish play.
Clean skeletons lay on the golden sand,
As I swim, seaweed washes through my hand.
Old chandeliers and gold-rimmed plates,
All these lie among broken crates.
Deeper and deeper I swim down,
Towards the hulk of rusty brown.
I see the ship so clearly now,
How did this ship sink? How?

Anna Lloyd-Williams (10)
Beaudesert Park School

My Mother's Handbag

Outside you are a boring leather cloud,
Inside you hold untold treasures,
An ancient notepad hides many forbidden secrets.
Hairbrushes are waiting like old hedgehogs.
Pens without lids are drying up.
Rusty old keys safe in her wallet.
Lipstick like a rolling barrel, cannons around.
Loose change tinkles about.
A new box of tissues are clean and white.
Concealed from the world, my mother's riches.

Natasha Neely (9)
Beaudesert Park School

Sisters

It was a Saturday morning,
The house was quiet,
My sister was up,
But why so quiet?

Just then, what a din,
My sister was boogieing!
She came in my room,
While singing 'Boom boom boom'.

She tripped over the dustbin,
What a din,
'Wake up sleepyhead,
Get out of bed!'

Mark Bates (9)
Beech Green Primary School

MY SISTER'S DOG

My sister has a dog
And Angel's his name
He wouldn't bite anyone
He's really quite tame

Angel likes his food
Especially mine
So when he scrounges
Mum keeps him in line

Don't be fooled by his name
He can be quite bad too
If you've got his toy
Be careful, I've warned you

He's quite big built
And extremely strong
When I take him on a walk
He pulls me headlong

At the end of the day
He's really quite sweet
I must admit it
Having a dog's neat.

Laura Rose Wilson (9)
Beech Green Primary School

MY BED

My bed is really high
It feels like I'm in the sky
Through the metal shiny bars
I can see the shooting stars.

Nathan Jones (10)
Beech Green Primary School

THE SILENT NIGHT

In the silent night
The wind is breezy and full of might
As I come to a bright light
I still have to fight
Through the silent night

I am stood by a wood
Trying to be silent as I stood
Being good as I should
Putting up my hood
In the silent night

In the woods I start to walk
I dare not talk
There I saw a silent fork
In the middle was a stalk
In the silent night

The woods have come to an end
Before too long I'll have to bend
And make my back quickly mend
Then therefore I will send
Goodbye silent night.

Shanice Taitt (10)
Beech Green Primary School

BATH

B   ath have got a rugby team
A   nd always had some skills,
T   he problem that Bath have now,
H   ow they pay their bills!

Blake Smith (9)
Beech Green Primary School

TIGER

Tiger, tiger, eyes gleaming bright,
You don't hunt in day but at the dark of night.
Teeth as sharp as razors,
Quietly from behind, you ambush your prey and bite
Its neck, to perform the mighty kill!

Tiger, tiger, gentle, kind and loving to its young,
Feeds it and cares for it too,
But soon, it will grow up and care for its own cubs
And to them it will be true.

Tiger, tiger, stripes so vivid and mild,
Its eyes as bright as sapphires,
Black and orange or black and white are your stripes,
Your nose as pink as grapefruit,
So if you ever see a tiger, lovely, gorgeous and bright,
It might be the tiger I'm talking about,
Who hunts at the dark of night.

Amy Voysey (8)
Beech Green Primary School

ANIMAL POEM

N   ewts are brown and scary,
A   ntelopes are hairy,
T   igers are fast and sharp,
H   ippos are big and chubby,
A   nts are small and fast,
N   its are dirty, crawling through someone's hair.

Nathan Barnett (10)
Beech Green Primary School

EGGS FOR EARS

I have eggs for ears
What am I talking about?
I have eggs for ears
I have bacon for my lips
What am I talking about?
I have eggs for ears
I have bacon for my lips
I have a sausage for my nose
What am I talking about?
I have eggs for ears
I have bacon for my lips
I have a sausage for my nose
I have tomatoes for my eyes
What am I talking about?

Alexandra McLaughlin (9)
Beech Green Primary School

I AM A PUDDLE

I   am a puddle with a ripple in the water

A   loving mother hugging her daughter
M   aybe a wild fire who loves to rage?

A   golden lion prowling around in its cage?

P   ossibly a nightingale who begins to fly,
U   nder the wonderful moonlit sky.
D   ancing snowflakes in the air,
D   id you see that fruit bowl? I was the pear!
L   ots of clocks telling the time,
E   ndings of poems with a very last rhyme.

Danielle Parker (10)
Beech Green Primary School

WEATHER

Winter can be cold,
Winter can be wet,
The first days of spring,
We look forward to get,
The first signs of growth,
That the warm welcome can bring.

The holiday season starts,
When we break up from school,
The hot, sizzling days,
We love to dive in the pool.
But as the summer season ends,
The wind begins to blow,
In the blustery days of autumn,
We huddle back in front of the fire,
In the warmth of its glow.

James Campbell (10)
Beech Green Primary School

THE DUMP

Rusty cars, sunken ships,
Lots and lots of apple pips.
Blown-up aeroplanes, screwed-up knives,
Lots of trains have lost their lives.
Teddy bears, cotton wool,
Wooden chair legs and a springy ball.
Dirty cookers, mouldy fridges,
Lots of parts of broken bridges.

Ashley Chadwick (9)
Beech Green Primary School

HIDDEN TREASURE

H ave you seen any treasure?
I t hides on the seashore,
D own under a lake, on top of a mountain.
D o you want to hear some more?
E veryone wants treasure,
N o one can resist!

T o find hidden treasure,
R ead a treasure map,
E veryone needs treasure
A nd there's no time for a nap.
S ure, it may be hard,
U nless someone's helping you.
R ow back with the treasure,
E veryone's jealous of you!

Jack Brown (10)
Beech Green Primary School

HIDDEN TREASURES OF THE SKY

Angels flying way up high,
Over the clouds in the pale-blue sky.
We see the angels up above,
Each and every one filled with love.

While flying with grace,
Dresses of lace,
They have hair like milk
And faces soft as silk.

These are our treasures of the sky,
Angels.

Kelly-Anne Griffiths (11)
Beech Green Primary School

CHILDREN

Children are funny
Children are silly
When I'm like this
My mum calls me silly billy

We like to play
We like to dance
We would get away with anything
If we had the chance

Some children are good
Some children are bad
My mum says I'm a good girl
Which makes me glad.

Keira Lowe (10)
Beech Green Primary School

DOLPHINS

D   olphins bow ride
O   ver that wave
L   eft there by your boat
P   eople admire them
H   iding with the others
I   n their special schools
N   ear the top of the
S   ea.

Stephanie Louise Fry (9)
Beech Green Primary School

SNAKE

Slithers through the gleaming ground,
As he coils up, round and round,
Opens his huge fangs
And executes his struggling prey.

He opens his blinding eyes
And spits and spits until he dies,
Camouflaged, living in the scorching desert.

He's like an enormous cheetah,
Slithering rapidly, as quickly as he can,
As he races through the rusty grass,
Next time you look, he won't be there.

Liam Swattridge (8)
Beech Green Primary School

007

J   ames likes to jazz
A   nd go for target range,
M   ashing all his villains,
E   xcept for Jaws
S   ome villains have deadly weapons.

B   lasting at the speed of light,
O   ver all the rooftops,
N   eeding his Walther PPK,
D   ancing with lots of girls.

Matthew Williams (9)
Beech Green Primary School

DOLPHIN

Splashing, sploshing,
Splattering in the sea,
A dolphin swimming,
He soars like a rocket,
Through bits of broken boats
And is followed by some fish.

The fish were multicoloured
And as dazzling as the stars,
Floating away, they heard Dolphin's cry,
But never went back, it was *danger*.

The dolphin soon hears a noise
And never makes a move,
The sound of people communicating,
Hears a big splash,
Gets caught by long rope
And bleeds with a cry!

Rachael Gough (9)
Beech Green Primary School

MONSTERS

Monsters, what are monsters?
Are they green with bright-red spots?
Have they got six stripey legs?
With four teaspoons as arms?
Have they got two golf balls as eyeballs?
Are their noses like triangles?
Do they have ears that wriggle?
Are their mouths like diamonds?

Claire Bromfield (10)
Beech Green Primary School

THE HIDDEN TREASURE

Somewhere on the golden beach
There is hidden treasure,
Maybe it is in a cave or under the sea,
But no, it is under the golden sand.

Soon I'll be rich,
Maybe, just maybe
I will live in a house of my own,
Golden walls, peach carpet
And lots more things,
No, I don't want to be rich
Or have a house of my own,
I like the way I am, with my family.

Callum Mark Gomersall (10)
Beech Green Primary School

SNAKE

Invisible, sneaky and sly,
The snake slides through a billion steeples.

The snake's eyes are gleaming crystals,
Eyes sharp to corner their prey.

Teeth as sharp as needles
And an excruciating sting.

The snake gulps like pouring water
And the snake has frightening speed.

Lee Merchant (9)
Beech Green Primary School

THE WITCHES' SPELL

First witch:
Intestines from a bat when landed in a tree,
Tail from a rat when roaming free,
Take some fur of a woolly sheep,
Put in while sitting fast asleep.
A big turtle's shell swimming in the sea,
A newt's tail, sting of bee.
Dragon's head, lizard's skin,
Then add barn owl's wing.

All:
Double, double, toil and trouble,
Fire burn and cauldron bubble.

Second witch:
Skin of lion, ear of rat,
Shark's teeth, wing of bat,
Put in a little tiger's nose,
Then some unicorn's toes.
Leg of bird, bullfrog's eye,
Dog's ear, wing of fly.

All:
Double, double, toil and trouble,
Fire burn and cauldron bubble.

Second witch:
With a touch of dragon's head,
Make sure he's very dead,
Don't forget a bear's paw,
Then add lion's claw.

Third witch:
Add six whiskers from a cat,
But make sure you don't drop in your hat.

First witch:
Add some colour with donkey's head,
Then you add the monkey's leg.

All:
In the end you will have a poison,
But make sure it kills that horrible person.

Lisa Raines (10)
Cam Everlands Primary School

THE WITCHES' SPELL

First witch:
Dirty vests, smelly socks,
Shorts and T-shirts; filthy frocks.
In the daytime nose of monk;
In the evening bark from trunk.
Then put in a dragon's claw;
Add to it a rabbit's jaw.

All:
Double, double, toil and trouble:
Fire burn and cauldron bubble.

Second witch:
At midnight add a queen bee's sting;
Then the powers of a kung-fu king.
Poison blood from Hydra's head;
Shell of egg from dinosaur's bed.
(Dead or alive) eye of newt;
Then a tail from a coot.

All:
Double, double, toil and trouble:
Fire burn and cauldron bubble.

Third witch:
Tiger's paw, in it goes,
Guinea pig's entrails and its nose.
When it's asleep, hair of bat,
With some scissors, ear of cat.

Add to it feather of owl,
Then put in a great wolf's howl.
Moss from a big sappy log,
Tusk from a fat hairy hog.

All:
Double, double, toil and trouble:
Fire burn and cauldron bubble.

Victoria Page (11)
Cam Everlands Primary School

THE WITCHES' SPELL

First witch:
Nose of bear and ear of cat.

Second witch:
Beak of bird, wing of bat.

Third witch:
Half-eaten rabbit, in it goes.

First witch:
Fingers, hands and feet with toes,
Leg of spider, wild wolf's howl,
Make it deadly, make it foul.

All:
Double, double, toil and trouble;
Fire burn and cauldron bubble.

Second witch:
Hamster's fur and rattle of snake,
All warmed up, ready to bake.
Skin of whale, a crab's claw,
Mix it up with pig's eyeball.
Donkey's foot, heart of frog,
Hand of man, tongue of dog.

All:
Double, double, toil and trouble;
Fire burn and cauldron bubble.

Third witch:
Heat it up, make it sour,
Then wait for half an hour.
After that, add a worm,
Hold it tight, don't let it squirm.
Add a black ant and a killer bee,
Add a bug and a squashed flea.
Just throw in a piece of copper,
Now the poison is good and proper.

Adam Wait (11)
Cam Everlands Primary School

THE WITCHES' SPELL

First witch:
A camel's brain from his head,
Will make the potion nice and red.
Add one pair of wild cat's eyes
And some grasshopper's antennas.
Put the ingredients in the pot,
Then we can get on with our plot.
Put in the dodo and the hare,
Now put in the skull of a bear.

All:
Double, double, toil and trouble;
Fire burn and cauldron bubble.

Second witch:
Put in the nose of a dog,
Add the spines of a hedgehog.
Throw some snow in to make it cold,
Now put in a little mould.
A long adder's big head,
Straight from its homely bed.
In goes a ladybird's wing,
Now put in a bumblebee's sting.

All:
Double, double, toil and trouble;
Fire burn and cauldron bubble.

Third witch:
Chop off a rabbit's tail,
Throw in the tongue of whale.
Put in a brown bear's head,
But just make sure that it is dead.
Throw in an antelope's toe
And a little grey rat's nose.

All:
Double, double, toil and trouble;
Fire burn and cauldron bubble.

Nathan Blick (11)
Cam Everlands Primary School

THE WITCHES' SPELL

First witch:
Rattle of snake, trapped in a door,
Crocodile's throat, found near the shore.
Crab's eyeball, caught asleep in a shell,
Bat's wing found by a church bell.
Zebra's brain, caught in the zoo,
Tiger's tooth about the size of you.

All:
Double, double, toil and trouble;
Fire burn and cauldron bubble.

Second witch:
Round and round the cauldron stroll,
Tail of a mouse, thrown into the bowl.
In goes the bird's big black wing,
Caught when it was just about to sing.
Stir in the redness of the goat's blood,
Leg of a spider, thrown in some mud.

All:
Double, double, toil and trouble;
Fire burn and cauldron bubble.

Third witch:
Mane of lion, stir it thick,
A shark's heart should do the trick.
In goes a wolf's big hairy ear,
A nice and small wet nose of deer.
A small but thick lizard's lung,
One more stir and the poison will be done.

Emily John (11)
Cam Everlands Primary School

THE WITCHES' SPELL

First witch:
Wool of sheep, a white snowflake,
Guts of snake, ready to bake,
Piglet's ear, put it here,
Sparrow's beak, very near.
Horse manure, cheetah's spots,
Add two broken china pots.

All:
Double, double, toil and trouble;
Fire burn and cauldron bubble.

Second witch:
Spider's web, monkey's tail,
Don't forget the fish's scale,
Dog's nose, rabbit's nails,
Now the insides of two fat snails.
Ladybird's urine, grinned cat,
Now we're ready for that chubby old gnat.

All:
Double, double, toil and trouble;
Fire burn and cauldron bubble.

Third witch:
Leg of horse, bat's wing,
Don't forget jellyfish sting,
Newt's skin, tiger's fur,
King and queen's blood; with myrrh,
Horse's leg, duck's padded feet,
Add a touch of donkey meat,
In goes the sparrow's nest,
Now your broth is ready to test.

Louise Hunt (11)
Cam Everlands Primary School

A POEM TO BE SPOKEN SILENTLY

It was so quiet that I heard;
a feather fall off a bird;
like someone breathing heavily.

It was so calm that I saw;
an atom get blown in the wind;
flying, floating sleepily, peacefully.

It was so silent that I heard;
the excitement flowing through the electricity wires;
dancing and partying all night long.

It was so still that I felt;
the air swirl around me;
like a twister taking over my body.

It was so peaceful that I heard;
the digging of a mole;
like a pneumatic drill.

It was so calm that I saw;
a flower opening up;
like a mouth chewing.

It was so quiet that I heard;
the hands racing around the clock;
speeding, sprinting.

Philippa McGlade (11)
Deerhurst & Apperley CE School

A Poem To Be Spoken Silently

It was so quiet you could hear an eye opening and closing,
dust moving through the air,
a ladybird scuttle across the grass,
a mouse squeak.

It was so quiet you could hear feet moving across the thick carpet,
petals fall off flowers,
a pencil writing,
raindrops falling.

It was so quiet you could hear a football being kicked,
a can drop,
a letter fall in the letterbox,
a spider spinning a web.

It was so quiet you could hear what you were thinking,
a page being turned,
a clock ticking,
somebody reading in their head.

It was so quiet you could hear goldfish eating,
cats purring,
dogs sleeping,
pigs breathing,
a rabbit's heart moving.

It was so quiet you could hear feathers in pillows,
the Earth moving.

Elena Mundy (11)
Deerhurst & Apperley CE School

A POEM TO BE SPOKEN SILENTLY

It was so quiet that you could hear the germs calling,
It was so quiet that you could hear the paper arguing,
It was so quiet that you could hear the sun glare on the Earth,
It was so quiet that you could hear the goalposts wobble in
                                        the calm breeze,
It was so quiet that you could hear the Earth turn its back on
                                        the blazing sun,
It was so quiet that you could hear the doors squeal like the
                                        weathervane spinning,
It was so quiet that you could hear the drawers rattle,
It was so quiet that you could hear the warmth rise up into
                                        the misty sky,
It was so quiet that you could hear the clouds stop the Earth
                                        from going haywire,
It was so quiet that you could hear the gutter mutter,
It was so quiet that you could hear the gates trying to free
                                        themselves from getting destroyed.

Ben Grundy (9)
Deerhurst & Apperley CE School

A POEM TO BE SPOKEN SILENTLY

It was so silent that I heard
a petal dying as it
fell from the flower peacefully

It was so silent that I heard
a caterpillar crawl up
the tree safely

It was so silent that I heard
memory of my
11th birthday with my friends and family

It was so silent that I heard
a worm crunching on an ant
which was dying a merciful death

It was so silent that I heard
a leaf opening to its
new life with its future ahead of it

It was so silent that I heard
a flame burst up a tree
in Australia.

Lorna Pike (11)
Deerhurst & Apperley CE School

A POEM TO BE SPOKEN SILENTLY

It was so quiet that I could hear the trees swishing and swaying.
It was so quiet that I could hear the wind crashing into the houses.
It was so quiet that I could hear a banana being peeled.

It was so quiet that I could hear a petal touching the ground.
It was so quiet that I could hear my mind being shocked in despair.
It was so quiet that I could hear the rubbery sound of a rubber.

It was so quiet that I could hear the sound of a feather fall from a bird.
It was so quiet that I could hear the sound of a snail crawling
                                                    on the ground.
It was so quiet that I could hear the whistling of the mole shuffler.

It was so quiet that I could hear a fish open his mouth and
                                                    shutting it again.
It was so quiet that I could hear the clock ticking and tocking.
It was so quiet that I could hear some dust falling from a lamp.

Abigail Stacey (10)
Deerhurst & Apperley CE School

A Poem To Be Spoken Silently

It was so quiet that you could hear the tooth fairy beating
her wings rapidly.
It was so quiet that you could hear a banana ripen itself, as it
smiled like a human.
It was so quiet that I heard a black hole sucking so hard that
it nearly burst.
It was so quiet that you could hear the tiles on the roof rattling
in the still air.
It was so quiet that I heard the radiator's water sloshing like the
water in an angry river.
It was so quiet that you could hear the bacteria cheering as it
multiplied in millions.
It was so quiet that I heard the buzzing of a watch as it celebrated
when the hour passed.
It was so quiet that you could hear a granny's skin wrinkle like
the water in a pond.
It was so quiet that I heard a seed germinate like a flower opening up.
It was so quiet that you could hear a supernova's anger as it exploded;
two billion light years away.
It was so quiet that I heard a snowflake fall from the clouds, way up
in the sky, so happily it danced all the way.

Philip Wiseman (9)
Deerhurst & Apperley CE School

A Poem To Be Spoken Silently

It was so quiet that I could hear the moon turn his head.
It was so quiet that I could hear leaves falling from the tree branch.
It was so quiet that I could hear the sun waking from a long sleep.
It was so quiet that I could hear the clouds drifting up in the sky.
It was so quiet that I could hear the planets turning.

It was so quiet that I could hear the weather changing.
It was so quiet that I could hear a feather falling from a bird.
It was so quiet that I could hear a hair fall from a dog's coat.
It was so quiet that I could hear a spider spinning.
It was so quiet that I could hear a hummingbird hum.

Jade Barlow (10)
Deerhurst & Apperley CE School

A POEM TO BE SPOKEN SILENTLY

It was so quiet that you could hear a pencil being carved like
wood being chipped.
It was so quiet that you could hear the disease squealing desperately
for something to poison.
It was so quiet that you could hear the disastrous calls from
a dying star.
It was so quiet that I heard the rolling-over of the tired Earth.
It was so quiet that you could hear the trampling of the ant colony.
It was so quiet that I heard a thought vanish from the precious mind.
It was so quiet that you could hear an emotion drifting away from
your watery eyes.
It was so quiet that you could hear the radiator booming out
its furious heat.
It was so quiet that you could hear the glue attaching itself to
the innocent paper.
It was so quiet that you could hear the grinning snow settle its
way onto a car.
It was so quiet that you could hear a deadly smile on a digger as it
strands the gravel under a building.

Richard Tattersall (10)
Deerhurst & Apperley CE School

A POEM TO BE SPOKEN SILENTLY

It was so quiet that I could hear mirrors reflecting
And even ants crawling back and forth,
So quiet you heard dust floating.

It was so quiet that I could hear electricity buzzing
And feathers drifting down to the floor,
So quiet you heard flies walking.

It was so quiet that I could hear hairs swaying
And leaves' growth beginning,
So quiet you heard smoke rising.

It was so quiet that I could hear the Earth spinning
And snakes slithering,
So quiet you heard grass swaying.

It was so quiet that I could hear my watch ticking
And paper shivering,
So quiet you heard thoughts thinking.

It was so quiet that I could hear satellites beeping
And even termites rustling,
So quiet you heard glue setting.

Josh Roberts (11)
Deerhurst & Apperley CE School

A POEM TO BE SPOKEN SILENTLY

It was so quiet that I heard the flickering of lightning in the
midnight sky
It was so quiet that I heard the brain thinking
It was so quiet that I heard ants shuffling around

It was so quiet that I heard the flowers opening
It was so quiet that I heard the sun setting
It was so quiet that I heard spiders going to bed

It was so quiet that I heard the caterpillars snoring
It was so quiet that I heard the trees whisper to each other
It was so quiet that I heard the stars talking in the sky

It was so quiet that I heard the whistling of the mole shuffle
It was so quiet that I heard a leaf falling off a plant
It was so quiet that I heard a feather fall off a bird

It was so quiet that I heard the car drinking the petrol
It was so quiet that I heard dust falling from a lamp
It was so quiet that I heard a stapler being used.

Steffie Eggermont (10)
Deerhurst & Apperley CE School

THE MOON

The moon, a screwed-up milk bottle cap
gleaming in the darkness.
A silver spark glinting on a blackened world.
The moon, one side showing,
the other hidden in a misty veil.
The night watchman with his silver lamp.
This is the moon.

Kyle Shearer (10)
Eastcombe Primary School

SCHOOL

'Where are those blinkin' math books?'
Shouts the teacher giving us all dirty looks.

'I'm sure I left them here yesterday.
Right here in this grey tray.'

'Under all your math worksheets
And all your stories you did in neat.'

'I think I've seen them' say very brave boys.
'In your tray with those two lost toys.'

'Goodness gracious boys, you're right'
Says the puzzled teacher going gradually white.

'I will hand out the sheets and then get on.
Don't be silly and stop talking John.'

This losing things routine goes on throughout the day,
When it comes to home time there's a shout 'Hurray!'

Megan David (10)
Eastcombe Primary School

THE MOON

The moon shines brightly
Through a misty haze
Ghostly and spooky
On a cold winter's night

The moon shines brightly
In a clear starry sky
Lighting the way
On a quiet summer's night.

Daniel Camm (9)
Eastcombe Primary School

MYSTERIOUS MOON

Mysterious moon sailing up high
What secrets do you hide?
You light up the darkening sky
And control the ocean tide.

They say moonlight is romantic
But can also be creepy,
Creating shadows in the darkness,
Which can scare and make you weepy.

Old sayings mentioned 'The man in the moon'
And said it was made of green cheese
Since man has landed on the moon
We have disregarded these.

The moon has several phases
Full moon, half and new.
A saying 'Once in a blue moon'
And of Earth a perfect view.

Rebecca Cairns (10)
Eastcombe Primary School

DARKNESS

In the twinkly moonlit garden,
I sat and looked up at the sky,
I looked at the shiny stars
And came across the mysterious moon.

I wonder what it's like up there?
I'd like to bounce lightly in a spacesuit,
Suddenly the moon goes behind a cloud
And I'm left in darkness.

Sam Mincher (8)
Eastcombe Primary School

THE MOON

Night is here
Look up
The shining, shimmering moon
Lightens up the sky
On a cold frosty night

The moon looks down
Seeing swooping owls
Hunting badgers
Stalking foxes
And scuttling mice

People sleep
Until the moon fades away.

Jennifer Adams (9)
Eastcombe Primary School

TROPICAL

Come and swim to my tropical island
Come and taste my wonderful fruits
Mangoes, bananas, grapefruit too
Now come and see my tropical island

Come to my tropical island
And you will find some wonderful things
Like playing on the golden sand until night
When the sun goes down

Now it is time to swim away
And come back another day.

Sam Reeves (11)
Eastcombe Primary School

AUGUST NIGHT

Cool now.
The sun goes down,
To feed the brown burnt lawn.
From pond to sprinkler, water
To grow.

Samantha Oakley (10) & Naomi Robbins (9)
English Bicknor CE Primary School

SPRING MORNING

Fresh start.
Buds are growing.
Birds singing, baby lambs
Playing in the fresh green grass.
New life.

Sarah Bland (10)
English Bicknor CE Primary School

NOVEMBER MORNING

Frosty,
Ice on the pond,
Christmas is getting close,
It's nearly too foggy to drive,
Winter.

Merlin Rowles (8)
English Bicknor CE Primary School

JANUARY EVENING

Darkness.
The blue blanket.
Cold air breathes upon me,
Like the breath of passing spirits.
Quiet!

Robyn Hunter (10)
English Bicknor CE Primary School

JANUARY MORNING

The hill
Sun rises up
Shadows form down below
Melting frost warming up people
New day.

William Osborne (9)
English Bicknor CE Primary School

JUNE NOON

Boiling
It's a great day
A blazing sun has come out
Summer holidays have come
Scorching.

Joshua Evans (8)
English Bicknor CE Primary School

MARCH MORNING

Sparkling.
Dew glittering,
Children having breakfast,
The postman whistling on his round,
Happy.

Miriam Hamilton (8)
English Bicknor CE Primary School

DECEMBER MORNING

Cold breeze
Sparkling ice dew
It will be New Year soon
It will start to get colder soon
New day.

Timothy Greenman (9)
English Bicknor CE Primary School

SPRING

Sunrise,
Birds twittering,
Baby animals come.
Butterflies flying in the wind,
New life.

Jessica Hone (10)
English Bicknor CE Primary School

OCTOBER EVENING

Sunset.
Leaves are falling.
The air is very cold.
Tonight's sky, full of orange clouds.
Darkness.

Lucy Rowles (10)
English Bicknor CE Primary School

AMERICAN NIGHT

Tearing.
It's like lightning,
Furious, dangerous.
It is a terrible killer.
Slicing.

Matthew Lacey (11)
English Bicknor CE Primary School

FROSTY NIGHT

Snowing,
Wind is blowing.
River flowing, ice glows.
How frosty can it really get?
Freezing.

Stephen Brown (9)
English Bicknor CE Primary School

AGONISING AUGUST NIGHT

Cooling.
It's getting dark.
Beautiful colours in
the sky. Now it is bedtime. I
can't sleep!

Martyn Blakemore (10)
English Bicknor CE Primary School

WHAT IS HIDDEN

Under the sea and down below,
Where the fish swish and sway,
There is a secret, a very big one
And no one will speak or say.

In a wrecked ship or under the sand,
I don't have a clue,
But somewhere, I don't know,
It is hidden in the depths.

I don't know what is guarding it,
Something mean and tough,
Like a shark or swordfish,
Something hard and rough.

OK, I'll tell you what it is,
As long as you don't tell,
Because it is a very big secret,
That's right, treasure.

Jay Delves (9)
Fairford CE Primary School

FRIENDS

Friends are people that care
Friends are always there
Friends keep secrets that you share
Friends come with you no matter where

They help you up when you fall
They come outside and play football
They're never horrible at all
They're always there for you to call

I don't care what they say
I don't care what they do
I don't care who they are
As long as they're my friend through and through.

Letty Indge (10)
Fairford CE Primary School

HORSES

Horses are pretty
Horses are nice
Horses are fun to ride
Horses are fast
Horses are grazing in the field
Horses are loving
Horses are eating hay
Horses are getting groomed
Horses are getting fed
Horses are galloping in the hills
Horses are charming.

Katie Correia (8)
Fairford CE Primary School

MY HIDDEN TREASURE

I have a hidden treasure,
That fills me with pleasure
And builds my heart throughout,
When I look,
I see a book,
On the floor
Is a round core,
It can be many colours
And shine through the others
That is behind the door,
It has a life
And is as sharp as a knife,
The birthstone never dies,
Unless I tell some lies.

Luke Martin (11)
Fairford CE Primary School

UNDER THE SEA

Deep beneath the ocean's cover,
Buried in the glistening sand,
There lies a mysterious wooden box,
I would love to open it someday,
Except it's blocked with heavy rocks,
I think I might be imagining this,
But I do believe it's true,
But later in your wildest dreams,
It might come true to *you!*

Alice Edwards (11)
Fairford CE Primary School

EARTH'S SECRETS

In the gloomy darkness,
Where the sun doesn't shine,
Something lays unknown,
To the world outside.

Slowly, so slowly it grows,
Underneath all of life.
A small treasure is forming,
Into something so bright.

Minutes, hours, days, months,
This secret treasure grows,
Making no sound at all,
While life moves on.

A small green shoot appears,
So young, new and fresh,
It will grow so steadily on,
Till a beautiful flower's made.

Becky Mumford (9)
Fairford CE Primary School

THE MOON

Climbing steadily into the evening sky,
On its journey it will fly,
Over the frosted mountain tops,
Slowly rising non-stop.

So its journey carries on,
Faster it dances as life moves on,
Its bleary, chalky white shape soars on more,
Its dazzling light shines through your open door.

Shyly the moon hides its face,
Gradually finding another place,
Soon the sun rises in the sky,
As the world continues going by.

Harriet-Jade Harrow (8)
Fairford CE Primary School

UNDER THE SEA

Under the sea, under the sand
You'll see me
Laying and glazing at the sandy land
You will see there is a light that leads you and me to a box you will see
Under the sandy land and under the blazing sea
There is a treasure box, I'm sure there'll be
With jewels and gold and cockleshells
On it there will be jingling bells

Under the sea, under the sand
In there will be silver and gold
And then you will behold
The treasures of the gold
Pebbles and cockleshells, there will be a land
Sell them, give them
So old and poor people can have some

Rich or poor, will be more
And my friend might share it with me
Please give so you will be famous
How generous and kind you will be
So go to the sea where cockleshells will be.

Susie Taylor (10)
Fairford CE Primary School

THE EARTH

He creeps along at dusk and dawn,
Circling his mother while she stands proud,
His crying tears run down his sweeping emerald gown,
For he leads a lonely life quite apart from his own world.

He only sees and hears his mother,
But never got so close to touch her,
She hopes to meet him, but he cannot come,
For fear of death,
Her house beholds a wisp of fire.

His father's clock shines loud at night,
While his mother sees the day so bright,
His brothers and sisters miles away, live their lives day by day.

Many others share his humble home,
But he stands tall shadowing them all,
The Earth is a treasure we'll never forget,
There is only one, so treat it well.

Rachael Burton (11)
Fairford CE Primary School

PENGUINS

Penguins sweet, penguins nice
They like to live on ice
In the morning they go for a swim
But you never see them yawning.

In the evening they lay down
And the little ones play around
But Mummy and Daddy stick around.

Luke Maunder (11)
Fairford CE Primary School

TREASURE CHEST

My brother has a treasure box,
With jewels of red and blue
And gold and silver pirate coins,
With a map covered in glue.

My brother has a treasure map,
With X that marks the spot
And two other Xs,
That try really hard to swap.

My brother has a pirate hat,
With a feather coming out the top
And a sort of white pirate skull,
Made out of lollipops.

My brother has a pirate ship . . .
This could go on forever.

Helen Gordon (11)
Fairford CE Primary School

A CAR

He runs down the lane,
Holding his passenger Whayne.
He swivels round the bend,
Growing near his end.
He gives way to his mate,
Turning right and going through the gate.
Whayne makes him do a wheelspin,
Then a man shouts, 'What's all that din?'
He turns left to go to the mall
And then he crashes into the wall.

Robin Taylor (10)
Fairford CE Primary School

MY DOG, MILLY

My dog, Milly is a little Yorkshire terrier,
She has a black coat
And a short little throat.
I take her for a walk
And throw her orange ball a mile,
She runs and runs,
For a little while.

She barks at the ducks,
The ducks quack back.
We walk on further
And look at the weather.
It starts to rain
And I think 'Oh what a pain.'
We race over the field and jump over the river,
We get back to our house, we're wet, we're cold, we shake and shiver.

Emma Yells (10)
Fairford CE Primary School

THE WIND

The wind is like a lonely call,
It sounds like someone is about to fall.
It's sometimes loud, sometimes soft,
I can hear it in my loft.
The wind blows the trees
And strips it bare of leaves.
The wind blows the washing,
It takes it off the line.
The wind can howl,
The wind can cry,
It often brings a tear to the eye.

Robert Coggins (10)
Fairford CE Primary School

THE ROSE

She beams all day at everyone,
Greeting them with her merry dance,
Sending joyful sparks out at them,
They become deeply entranced.

In the evening she wears her best sparkling gown,
Scarlet in colour with verdant stilettos,
Swirling and twirling, merrily laughing,
She elegantly appears.

On a summer's morning,
She bobs up and down,
Laughing and joking with her neighbours,
They say she should wear a glimmering crown.

You may have guessed who I'm talking about,
She lives quite nearby,
You may have laughed with her before,
Her name is Rose, but why?

Hannah Embleton-Smith (10)
Fairford CE Primary School

SOMETHING PRECIOUS

When someone says the word 'Precious' I always think of my dog.
She means more to me than anything, forever I'll always love her.
To me, she's not an animal, she's a person with feelings too.
If she ever was to die, I don't know what I'd do.
Treasure to me is a load of rubbish compared to my dog, Sasha,
She's pretty, sweet and cute! No dog will ever be better!

Gemma Clarke (11)
Fairford CE Primary School

MY POEM

All I ask
is a perfect day
on a perfect beach
in a perfect bay
in the perfect shade
of a perfect tree
with a perfect view
of a perfect sea
with a perfect breeze
and a perfect sky
read a perfect book
swat a perfect fly
in a perfect pool
find a perfect shell
eat a perfect peach
with a perfect smell
skim a perfect stone
dig a perfect hole
catch a perfect wave
score a perfect goal
make a perfect drive
see a perfect fish
with a perfect tail
give a perfect swish
then in this perfect world
meet a perfect friend
and bring this perfect day
to a perfect end.

Holly Parker (8)
Fairford CE Primary School

MY DOG

He is a feisty little thing,
Who chews up your stuff.
He's a troublesome pest,
But he is very much loved.

He chases his tail,
From dawn to dusk.
He is a typical male,
Just can't get enough.

Cute little puppy,
With deep brown eyes.
He likes jumping in water,
Even if ice.

Georgia Alice Hastings (10)
Fairford CE Primary School

LIFE OF THE SEA

The sea crashes,
The sea tumbles,
Waves rising, gliding,
Then colliding.

But . . . down in the deep,
Where the fishes sleep,
A world on its own,
Where the waves shan't moan.

But meanwhile on top,
There are waves which will never stop,
The water goes on howling and howling.

Sian Parnell (10)
Hardwicke Parochial Primary School

THE SEA

I picked up a shell
And what did I hear?
The wonderful sound of the sea
I closed my eyes and dreamt a dream
Of waves lapping over me

I picked up a shell
And what did I hear?
The swish and the swoosh of the waves
Crashing over the rocks, old and worn
The tide rushing into the caves

I picked up a shell
And what did I hear?
Nothing, the sea was calm and clear
The sand gleaming like gold in the sun
All the children having fun

Mum picked up a shell, it sounded like the sea
I picked up a broken shell, trust me!

Amy Williams (11)
Hardwicke Parochial Primary School

THE SEA

The sea, very much like an angry girl,
Always worrying about her lovely hair,
When it's a mess, the waves crash,
For all of us to bear.

When it's neat, the waves are calm,
Just like a soft teddy bear,
But when it's wet, it looks like a velvet shadow,
Just lying lonely there.

Then softly the tide comes in,
Close for all to see,
Just like the little girl,
Whose hair has had the best style ever to be.

With the safety of her soft little ted,
She takes her bear to bed,
She dreams about the sea with thoughts,
The beauty, the frights and the wonders of the ocean bed.

Jessica Hynes (10)
Hardwicke Parochial Primary School

THE MUSIC BAND

As it rolls on the sand,
Sounding like a music band,
Rushing up once again,
Filling a child's sandpit den!
Cliffs so near, steep and tall,
With a sudden drop, quite a fall!
Trees on the pasture,
Safe from the sea,
With the pebbles,
Trying to flee!
Seagulls soaring
Through the sky,
Over the sandy beach,
Now quite dry!
Bathers jumping off the boats,
Jellyfish surfacing, see them float,
As it rolls on the sand,
Rushing up, once again . . .

Ethan Wilkinson (11)
Hardwicke Parochial Primary School

THE CHANGING SEA!

The sea is like an angry white horse
That eats and grinds the salt and meat
Of human beings and human feet
That run up the beach to safety.
The waves are crashing, tumbling, roaring,
Crashing upon rocks in the sea,
Unsafe for even the smallest flea,
So don't risk your life just run.
Some people collect the shells that it leaves,
The ones that the sea has forgotten,
Left behind when the tide had to run,
'Cause the tide had to change and go.
The angry white horses
Go in and go to their beds,
They rest their sleepy heads,
Beware, we'll be out on a windy day.

Mary Edwards (11)
Hardwicke Parochial Primary School

THE SEA

The sea's eternal loyalty to man and beast alike,
Is of such great sincerity it keeps us all alive,
We live so much more happily with water than without,
So do not take for granted our abundant sea amount,
For it will soon be gone if it is used at such a speed,
So let us work together to conserve our useful seas,
Let's make a life worth living with the lovely old sea breeze,
So in a thousand years or so, we'll still enjoy the sea.

Joe Alderman (10)
Hardwicke Parochial Primary School

THE SEA DOG!

It's a dark, cold, crisp night
And there's a small boat in view's sight,
Then a storm comes, arouse
And the cloud allows
The sea dog to gnaw upon the *boat!*
The morning has come and all is well,
The sea is clear, clear as a bell,
But the sorrow of the night is still in blight,
As the dog knows he is not right . . .

The time has begun for the shine of the sun,
To downpour on the sea.
With a glistening eye,
It catches the sight of children nearby,
They play and splash, while the waves still lash and lash.

Jasmine Dalmeny (10)
Hardwicke Parochial Primary School

THE SEA

The sea, an angry mob of waves, smashing and crashing,
Bony, white fingertips catching the lifeless sand,
Stones are hurtled towards cliff edges,
Sea creatures are thrown into the cold, sharp air.

Tossing the fisherman's boat from side to side,
Seagulls hiding in their dens from the frightful surroundings,
Fishes try to swim to the safe seabed like bullets out of a gun,
A tall thin building guiding ships away from the knife-like rocks.

Ross Howell (11)
Hardwicke Parochial Primary School

WHAT IS THE SEA?

The sea is a rough orang-utan,
Giant marine colours it frowns,
He hops down the beach at morning,
He jumps up the beach after dark.
Hours and hours he rolls on the bay,
Rumbling all the stones away,
Food, food, food,
The giant sea monkey moans
And when the wind rose high,
The sea monkey cried,
Louder than his normal sound,
The sound is deafening; loud and clear.
But in the summer,
The monkey is calm,
No longer he moans, runs and groans,
The monkey is a monster, rough and tough.

Ian Hawksworth (10)
Hardwicke Parochial Primary School

LIFE IN THE SEA

Splashing and clashing on the rocks
The tide was coming in, washing bones and weed
Birds were looking down at the sea
Hoping that they would find some food on the sea bay

Waves like tall hills and people walking on the sand
A storm was rising
As the day went on
The tide went back, wishing it had more fun.

Rebecca Bamford (10)
Hardwicke Parochial Primary School

DOWN BY THE SEA

Down by the sea you can have the best time,
in the morning when all the ships are in line.
The children come down to the sand
and race and race and race around.
They play, it's so much fun for everyone . . .
It's time for the picnic on the cliffs
and up above the wind is so swift.
We have our picnic, cakes and crisps,
the basket was too heavy for anyone to lift.
The sea below was crashing around,
making the most noisiest sound.
We raced back down by the sea,
but we only found a few shells on the ground . . .

Harriet Higgins (10)
Hardwicke Parochial Primary School

THE SEA!

The sea gets closer, tickling my toes,
My dog has a sniff, gets salt up his nose,
The sea starts to throw pebbles and stones,
I walk along the beach with an ice cream cone.

Then there's a crash, a bang and a roar,
I look up above, see the gulls soar,
The clouds are gathering, the sky's getting black,
The sea's getting angry, I need to move back.

I shout for my dog, he comes at a run,
The sea starts to chase us, I fall on my bum,
The waves get higher, there's sand in my eyes,
A mouthful of sea water, what a nasty surprise!

Stacey Morgan (11)
Hardwicke Parochial Primary School

THE OCEAN BLUE

The sea is white horses
Stampeding onto the beach
Crushing, grinding
Crashing on the ground
Making a din

The sea is calm
Still and quiet
Not making the slightest splash
Not even in the
Misty distance

The sea is swimming
Swimming with fish
While fishers fish
The fish try to escape
And swim away

The sea is strong
As strong as steel
Making splashes
Splashes that are hammering
Hammering the metal

The sea is cold
As cold as ice
It makes everyone shiver
Shiver in fright
And it grows colder
Colder at night

The sea is angry
Wild and stormy
Crashing on the bend
Waiting for people to play
And have fun with the waves.

Jordan Rouse (10)
Hardwicke Parochial Primary School

SUNSHINE SUMMERS AT THE SEA

When the sea crashes
it makes lots of splashes
the little children play in the waves
lifeguard look, someone needs to be saved

When the tide goes back out
all the tourists moan and shout
oh well, we'll go and have some tea
make sandcastles and play in the sea

Locals go to a shop and get some rock
like a tasty cylinder stone, they lie on the beach
collecting shells kids can reach
and look at the pretty colours like a beautiful rainbow
shining bright whilst other kids fly a kite

Kids are racing on donkeys
make sure you don't fall off Leigh
later on they go home for an ice bun
and be back next summer for more beach fun

The best part is playing in the sea
you never know what it may be
a gigantic lion or a tiny little mouse
they all live in the ocean house.

Kelly Marie Fryer (11)
Hardwicke Parochial Primary School

THE FIRST STORM

The sea was once quiet and calm,
We went to swim and came to no harm,
We played all day, morning till night,
So when the storm came, we had a huge fright.

It shook about the salt and sand,
Messing and wetting the beachy sand,
It killed the crabs, whales and sharks,
Splashing the rocks, leaving big marks.

It lasted days and when it was fine,
It wasn't the same, the sun didn't shine,
We went to surf and ski and sail,
But swam off when we spotted a whale.

Even today, the sea is rough,
But we think it's good enough,
Playing in rough sea is for me,
But I'll never forget our quiet, calm sea.

Emily Mar-Gerrison (11)
Hardwicke Parochial Primary School

THE SEA'S JOURNEYS

The beach was lonely, deserted and dry,
waiting for waves of the sea to come by,
hoping to moisten each grain singled out,
for a roar of liquid to rush in with a shout.
But soon, salt water began to rush in, near,
seeping through the sand, each small, tiny tear,
but now it begins to fade and rush out,
carrying sand like through a teapot spout.

For each grain a new adventure about to begin,
taking it somewhere new to be buried in a den,
for the sea each second never filled with sand
and the same routine to look forward to tomorrow,
swimmers and divers, some lie on the beach,
lingering around for the sea to reach,
so soon people leave and the night draws near,
and the sea and the beach are once again clear!

Samuel Jellyman (10)
Hardwicke Parochial Primary School

THE SEA

Down at the beach one sunny day
That's when the sea comes out to play
Smashing, crashing all day long
Until the seagulls hum their song
Then the sea lies still and calm
Then the farm cockerel gives an alarm

Smashing, crashing once again
Fishes swim ten by ten
Dolphins are starting to swim
Until the day is dim
The sea is calm
Sea life no harm

Down on the beach one sunny day
That's when the children come to say
Thank you Jesus for this day
Now I want to go and play
Thank you Jesus for the sea
Everyone can play in it, like Eve and Cara-Leigh.

Cara-Leigh Taylor (10)
Hardwicke Parochial Primary School

THE DEEP BLUE SEA

The deep blue sea
Can be dangerous, can be fun
Treat it with respect and enjoy it in the sun
You can swim, surf or sail
Or relax on the beach with your spade and pail

The deep blue sea
Crashes on the sand
We are at a safe distance
When we watch from the land
The waves are strong, the waves are high
Underneath is where the seashells lie

The deep blue sea
Is calm at night
Letting the creatures curl up tight
The boats quietly sail away
As it's the end of the day

The deep blue sea
Is where the sea creatures live
The sharks take and the dolphins give
The fish swim, the jellyfish float by
While the seagulls fly high in the sky

The sun has set
The sea is wild
As wild as a loose dog
Grabbing everything
Taking everything
Back into the deep.

Emma Higgins (10)
Hardwicke Parochial Primary School

THE SEA

The sea is an ice-breathing dragon,
that whips with its ice-white tail
and attacks anything in its territory
and moves quickly,
especially through the pebbled seabed.

As sun sets, all is calm,
but as he wakes
to a very loud alarm,
it gets louder and louder,
he's very angry.

The dragon's whirling and whirling
and sucks everything in,
then spits it out and says 'Ugh, disgusting!'

Adam Cox (10)
Hardwicke Parochial Primary School

THE BIG BLUE SEA

The sea is so big, it goes on for miles and miles,
As the beach looks on, it smiles and smiles.
Until the waves beat down on the sandy rug,
Sandcastles and buildings that have been dug.
Fall, fall as memories from the day die,
The beach like a baby starts to cry.
The sea is like a giant spade,
As it hits down sandcastles people have made.
The beach is like a cat,
While the sea is a dog chasing just like that.
The sea can be either cold or warm,
But it's really cold in a frightful storm.

Daniel Sutton (11)
Hardwicke Parochial Primary School

THE STORMY SEA

The storm is like a madman lashing and raging out,
Bolts of lightning flashing through the sky.

Black clouds blotting out the sky like ink,
Grey waves towering as high as mountains,
Crashing and smashing together.
The fog shrouding off everyone's view,
A boat being tossed off course like a piece of driftwood,
Its crew like drowned rats.
Buoys bobbing up and down in distress straining at their anchor,
Seagulls trying to reach the shore, struggling against the air current,
No longer in control of their wings.

The tempest is over, the sea is once again quiet,
Blue fluffy clouds racing overhead,
The boat sails back to port, a gentle breeze fluttering its sails,
Screeching seagulls flying off the cliffs,
They swoop down like eagles to catch their watery prey,
Peace has returned to the shores.

James Parry (11)
Hardwicke Parochial Primary School

THE WHALE TALE

The whale in the darkness
Swimming on its belly
The rough tide carrying the whale on its way
The tide brings the whale on the shore
Stranded on the rough yellow floor
The tide as it gets rougher clashes down
Carrying the whale out to sea

As the fin hits the surface
The splashing of water drops like rain
As the whale suddenly screeches in pain
As it disappears under the sea
A single seagull flies in the sky
Coming from the sea, hearing the cry
As the whale swims on its way again.

Becky Chapman (10)
Hardwicke Parochial Primary School

BESIDE THE SEASIDE

Down on the beach where history lays,
Up on the bridge where people gaze.
Souvenir shops for you to see,
Come on, follow me.
Walk down the beach . . . on the bumpy hills,
Look through the lighthouse window sills.
The vicious waves crash against the rocks,
The little boats shaking in the docks.
Look at the sea coming over to me,
A pale blue mixed with a hint of cup of tea.
Seaweed and litter mixed into one,
Careful Kelly, I can see your bum!
The seagulls soar in the sky,
As I watch the day go by.
The sea was salty, the sand was pure,
The sky was pale cotton wool.
As I watch the day go by,
It brings a tear to my eye
To have to say, goodbye.

Kiya Marshall (11)
Hardwicke Parochial Primary School

ANGRY OR CALM?

The sea can be angry or it can be calm
The waves so large try to swirl and sway
Mostly when it's a stormy day
They keep trying and trying every day
It's the same again, again and again

The sea can be angry or it can be calm
The sea is quiet, flowing gently on the shore
Mostly when the sun comes forward
The sea stops trying, no crashing ever again
Again it's the same, again and again

The sea lies still and then the waves start falling
It's so unpredictable there's a chance of it storming
It will keep roaring forever more.

Daniel Griffin (10)
Hardwicke Parochial Primary School

OCEAN WAVES!

The crashing waves smashed against the tall, deep and
                                        everlasting beach,
Covered with silk, pebbles that shone in the sun.
The waves rising like a volcano getting ready its lava to spill.
The crashing waves explore the sand, deeper and deeper,
                                        round and round.
At last nightfall comes, still, still, around, around.
Nowhere for the sea to be found.
The sea disappears slowly, the distance in sight.
Slowly, slowly like watching an ice cube melt into a fizzy drink.
See all the crashing waves being pulled back for other days.

Laughna Morris (11)
Hardwicke Parochial Primary School

THE DEEP BLUE SEA

The sea glistens as the sun shines down
Waves splash on the rocks all around
Seagulls overhead squawk and scream
As people walk along eating ice cream

The beach of warm golden sand
With many models all built by hand
Children like fishes play in the sea
Until it's time to go home for tea

The sea is a millpond as night falls
No more people, sandcastles or beach balls
All is quiet, everyone's gone home for the day
Until tomorrow when they'll be back to play

It's a wonderful place to be.

Chelsea Jones (10)
Hardwicke Parochial Primary School

THE TREASURES OF THE WORLD

All the treasures of the world are hidden inside of you
All the treasures of the world are hiding, waiting for you
The delicate flowers of ice on the windowpane
The rainforest hides his treasures from you
From the fossils to the frogs, from the bee to the beaver
We all hold hidden treasures
And if you find one hidden in you
I hope you'll share it with us.

Lily Witchell (8)
Hopelands School

MAMMALS AT SEA

Mammals at sea
Dolphins
Whales
I like to see

Big ones
Small ones
Baby ones too

I like
Grey ones
White ones
Especially the blue

They love the sea
But they need
To breathe the air
Under or over
The water
They live there.

Chanelle Jones (9)
Hopelands School

THE WRECK

In an empty sea,
The huge wreck falls,
Nothing to do but fall.
Fishes swim in and out,
An empty sea,
An empty wreck.

Tables, chairs,
In a corner in a room a chest lies,
Not disturbed unless,
Divers come,
Looking for wrecks and treasures,
It may not be what they see.

Sophie McDonald (8)
Hopelands School

OCTOPUS

Octopus, octopus
Under the sea
Why do you hide your
Treasure from me?
The gold rings
The silver coins
Please tell me where
You hide the chest
Then I'll make you
The best

Octopus, octopus
Why do you hide?
Has someone in
Your family died?
The sparkling diamonds
The long chains
I hope you don't
Have any pains.

Phoebe Rodgers (8)
Hopelands School

HIDDEN TREASURES IN MY MIND

Hidden treasures in my mind
waiting just for me to find

In my mind I can see
pirates going to sea

Pirate flag flying well
and cannon ready to fire
treasure chest full, hidden in their ship

To find my hidden treasure
just waiting for me

There in the blue they disappear
then suddenly they reappear

But strangely enough
in the air

And there they stay
waiting for me to get my treasure today.

Alexandra Radcliffe (8)
Hopelands School

IMAGINING

I'm riding on my rollerblades
I'm flying through the air
I'm riding on my rollerblades, I haven't got a care
I'm going forwards over bumps, feeling very grand
I'm going through the wilderness to a magic land
The magic land is silver, the magic land is cold
And when I open my eyes again the magic land is gone!

Megan Smyth (9)
Hopelands School

SPOOKY MANSION

One stormy night in bed
I sleep
I hear the monsters around me creep
I hear them shout, I hear them bark
I see their eyes twinkle in the dark
I crept downstairs, I lifted the latch
And opened the door
I ran outside and hid in the den
Already there was my best friend, Ben
'Ben, how did you get there?'
'Monsters chased me down the stairs'
We saw a sparkle behind the hedge
We
Crawled
Underneath the prickly hedge
And there we saw our
Hidden treasure.

George Perrins (9)
Hopelands School

THE SEA

The wind was howling through the stormy sea
As I sailed my boat round
The wind and waves rushing on the sand
The cool blue and swirling round the rock
I look around at the calm gentle sea
Suddenly!
I saw a glint
What could it be?

Esther Gooch (8)
Horsley CE Primary School

THE GALE

The gale is like a shark
Attacking the land,
Biting off bits of fence and roofs,
Or a horse crushing trees with its giant hoofs,
Or a bird blowing people away with its beating wings.

The screeching sound as the wind sings,
Cars tossed in the air then coming down with a crash,
Blowing away all the trash,
Making mischief in the air,
Shutting down the local fair.

Making sure everything's messed,
Then turns away and disappears over the crest,
Looking with disbelief,
Then people breathe a sigh of relief,
Then turn round to clear the mess,
Now it's time to have a little rest.

Harry Tate (10)
Horsley CE Primary School

AUTUMN TIME

Leaves turning colour,
Falling off the trees,
People put more clothes on,
Autumn time is here.

Squirrels bury their nuts,
Birds migrate to warmer lands,
Gold leaves lie in the lane,
Trees bare all season,
Autumn time is here.

James Ashton (10)
Horsley CE Primary School

THE WOLF OF THE GALE

It's a ten force gale,
Look out! Here it comes.
It is an invisible wolf,
Never to fail!
Knocking over dustbins,
Rushing down roads,
Looking for something
To break with its powerful paws,
To clamp with its mighty jaws.
It has the power to knock over trees,
Blow over people,
Send lids dangerously around,
Making hardly any sound.
Pouncing in circles,
To get its prey,
To make the sea hurl its spray.
Twirling, swirling, whirling,
It's a ten force wolf gale,
Look out! Here it comes!

Bertie Barr (9)
Horsley CE Primary School

NATURE

Flowers twinkling with the morning dew,
Freshly sprouted, bright and new.
A spring day, a summer day, the cows give a moo.
Four-leafed clover and the spring of grass underfoot,
Sparkling water where a black cat stood,
At the water's edge on that day,
Daisy chains, bursting buds and a horse's neigh.

Sophie Forster (9)
Horsley CE Primary School

AUTUMN TIME

The leaves are fluttering once again,
It's autumn time, the colours of the leaves are golden and crimson,
Rustling in the wind.
Don't forget it's autumn.

The sun setting high in the sky,
Melting like an orange coin spreading on the horizon.
The gentle breeze just floating by,
Don't forget it's autumn.

The fields are all covered in golden corn,
Ready to be chopped at dawn.
The corn has been chopped and is made into flour,
Don't forget it's autumn.

Alfie Godden (10)
Horsley CE Primary School

THE GALE

The wind howled to the moon,
It pawed its sharp claws,
It pounded, at the trees it gnaws,
Like a hungry dog, mean and cold.

Then it roars, sending everything scattering,
It plays with the town,
Shaking it, rocking it, up and down,
Like a hungry dog, mean and cold.

It cries and moans,
The river bubbles and flows,
The wind, harder it blows,
Like a hungry dog, mean and cold.

Ellie Roberts (10)
Horsley CE Primary School

THE THING

The thing . . .
 Its curling claws reaching out to grab you.
 As you run away you can hear its long howl behind you.
The thing . . .
 Running over the morning dew,
 Coming, coming to get you.
The thing . . .
 Its stripy, glowing eyes take control of your mind,
 You follow it to its ghastly castle,
 Taking you, taking you far, far away from your home.
The thing . . .
 Feeds on your blood, every sip gives it more power,
 More life, so it lives forever!

 That thing you never want to see!

Charlotte Lee (9)
Horsley CE Primary School

HORSE RIDING

Horse riding is hard,
Not easy, but hard.
Jumping, galloping,
Trotting, walking and cantering.

Horses are slow
And very steady,
Soft-furred.
Like a carrot?
Yes!

Sophie Louisa Craven (8)
Horsley CE Primary School

AUTUMN IS HERE

The green leaves have gone,
now the crimson and brown leaves have come.
The autumn is here,
the winter is near
and still the autumn goes on.

The light blue sky has gone,
the wispy clouds have come.
The autumn is here,
the winter is near
and still the autumn goes on.

The gold corn has gone,
the hay bales have come.
The autumn is here,
the winter is near
and still the autumn goes on.

The hedgehogs have gone,
the robins have come.
The autumn is here,
the winter is near
and still the autumn goes on.

Kieran Colvin (9)
Horsley CE Primary School

THE BUZZARD

Prince of the skies,
Oaken-feathered,
Dagger beak,
Wild and weathered.

Wing of wood,
Golden eye,
Talons of steel,
Soaring high.

Rachel Savage (11)
Horsley CE Primary School

THE FALL OF SNOW

The night began when all was silent,
Then quite suddenly a gust of wind showered down upon the ground
And sprayed the Earth with gleaming white snow.
It covered the world in a twinkle of light,
All through the night, all was white.
The moon gleamed and seemed
To look like a coin,
It shimmered bright, with light.

Lindsay Allen-Hynd (10)
Horsley CE Primary School

THE GALE

The gale is an angry wolf,
trying to catch his prey,
he dashes down the street,
wrecking everything in the way.
He slashes houses with his claws
and people he will slay.
So, watch out everybody,
the gale is on its way.

Rosie Jade Jenkins (10)
Horsley CE Primary School

AND STILL THE AUTUMN WENT ON

Gold and crimson the leaves have now turned,
The colours whispered their song to the wind,
The bare trees shivered as the last leaf fell
And still the autumn went on.

The hedgehogs are in hibernation,
The badger finds a place to sleep too,
While the foxes are out in the racing wind
Wondering what to do
And still the autumn went on.

Now the fields are full with light,
The corn in the field has grown tall
And leaves in and out of the corn
And still the autumn went on.

Kelly Wright (9)
Horsley CE Primary School

THE EGG

Look! A hole and a crack,
The mother stands back,
Black eyes gleam,
For now it seems
Her child shall be born,
Wet and forlorn.
A cheep and a click –
It's happened so quick!
Out falls the duck's child,
Helpless and mild.

Hannah Fullard (11)
Horsley CE Primary School

AUTUMN LEAVES

Gold and crimson the leaves have now turned,
The colours whispered their song to the wind,
The bare trees shivered as the last leaf fell
And still autumn went on.

The hedgehogs are hibernating in their holes
As the cold wind rushes past,
Robins singing to greet you for the cold is coming,
Foxes rummaging about the ground for the time is running out
And still autumn went on.

Then came the day when nights were very cold
And every creature was in its warm not cold hole.
The first morning came when there was frost,
That was the first day of winter.

Oliver Huggett-Wilde (9)
Horsley CE Primary School

AUTUMN

Hedgehogs start their long autumn sleep,
Badgers dig a large deep burrow,
Dormice snuggle in a blanket of orange and golden leaves,
Foxes run from a large autumn breeze.

Farmers collect in harvest crops,
Apples, pears and other food,
Gathered in for winter,
A celebration in front of a sunset sun.

Charlotte Oatley (10)
Horsley CE Primary School

AUTUMN POEM

Gold and crimson the leaves have now turned,
The colours whispered their song to the wind.
The bare trees shivered as the last leaf fell
And still the autumn went on.

The hedgehogs have just started their hibernation,
All the foxes out and about finding food.
The badgers all snuggled up to their babies for a good night's sleep
And still the autumn went on.

The farmer stands in his fields and waits for the crops to grow,
When the crops are fully grown the farmer starts to pick the crops.
He has a lot to pick
And still the autumn went on.

The sky is full of beautiful fluffy clouds,
The sky has lots of nice colours.
The sky has a nice sun that shines up in the sky
And still the autumn went on.

Emma Dean (10)
Horsley CE Primary School

SUMMER DAYS

Buzzing bees
Teasing sun
Sizzling barbecues
Wrapped in a bun

Dry grass under your feet
While wrapping yourself in a wet sheet.

Amber LeGay (10)
Horsley CE Primary School

SLUGS, SLUGS

Crawling round the grass,
Watching the day go round.
Seeing all the bugs creeping past.

Caterpillar, caterpillar,
Long-legged, camouflaged bugs
Are crawling through the leaves,
Smelling all the smelly rugs
That are seeped through the sleeves

Bees, bees
Black and yellow, buzzing around,
They are making funny sounds,
Moving round and round.

Molly Wright (8)
Horsley CE Primary School

THE WHITE SNOW LADY

Snow covered in a silky white dress,
floated in the midst of the sky.
Smoked out a cold breath of air,
then whispered, 'Watch out children,
I'm coming down.'

She dropped down from the clouds above
and covered herself over the world in a blanket of snow.
The children down below screamed, 'Yippee'
and scattered her all around.

Kathryn Savage (9)
Horsley CE Primary School

UNDER MY BED

Mum's old Horse and Hound rolled up to swat flies,
A sticky old Chewit covered in straw,
5p, I hoped it would be more,
A couple of hamster droppings,
Oh, there's the hamster,
Come on, back in your cage.
My school sock, a Game Boy game,
50p, that's better!
Callum's French prep, all crumpled and creased.
A stale old pizza crust,
A roll of Sellotape.
Mum, where's the Hoover?

Bryony Smith (8)
Ingleside School

WATER

Calm seas flowing to the ocean
Torrential rain blasting down
Soothing baths healing wounds
Home to fish
Gushing out of mountains
Making waterfalls
Fun to splish and splash in summer
Fun to skate and ski in winter
Jumping in puddles with brightly-coloured wellies
Making trees and plants grow upwards to the light
Essential to life.

James Hale (8)
Ingleside School

THE RIVER

Through the countryside speeds the river
With its cooling waters it will make you shiver
It's such a lovely place to go out
Let's go fishing and catch some trout
We will row a boat
I will swim with you and my water float
Please, oh come on, let's go
I want to see the river flow
I want to hear the spraying of the foam
I do not want to stay at home.

Amelia Wreford (8)
Ingleside School

HORSES

Shining forelock
Mane rippling
Tail streaming in the wind
Glinting hooves
Galloping over the moors, snorting hot breath over everything
Saddle reflecting the sunlight
Reins clutched in rider's hands
While fearlessly driving his steed.

Emily Blampied (8)
Ingleside School

WILLOW TREE

Willow tree with drooping branches
Reflects the moonlight in its boughs
Curtain of green blowing and blowing
While two lovers sit and watch it ripple the water.

Madeleine Turner (9)
Ingleside School

DEEP UNDER

Deep under the water I dive,
To treasure, gold and corals blue.
Deep under the water I skive,
Skive away from school.

I search for treasure, long forgotten,
Tapestries, china, all to be gotten.
Mounds of helmets, steel and tin,
Tons of logbooks all about our kin.

Animals, colours all around me,
Swimming and gaping at the sea.
Plants that before I could only dream,
All behaviours, friendly and mean.

Further, further down I go,
To touch the bottom as a crow.
Soaring and swooping lower and lower,
I glide and move slower and slower.

I kick and pull up and up,
Forgetting all pretence of being a crow.
All I want is to get out,
Of this dark, dark below.

As I furiously surge upwards,
My hand connects on something.
Somebody whispers in my ear,
'You want treasure old, I hear.

But please take this,
To remember our sea with'
And places into my palm,
The ocean's ten psalms.

Never ever from that day on,
Did I sing of treasure or be forlorn,
Because I know now, I knew then,
I've got the greatest treasure, ever given to men.

Laura Kate Mansbridge (11)
Kingswood Primary School

A TREASURED MOMENT

It's not a ruby,
It's not a sapphire,
It's not a pearl,
It's not a jewel.

It's not gold,
It's not silver,
It's not bronze,
It's not money.

It's not man-made,
It's not from the Earth,
It's not noisy,
It's not quiet.

It's purer than a unicorn,
Purer than spring water,
Purer than the untouched snow
And it's purer than a diamond.

It's the sorrowful stare of the naughty puppy
And the softening expression from Mum.

Lauren Aldridge (10)
Kingswood Primary School

HIDDEN TREASURE

One day when I was walking along,
I tripped on something hard,
I wondered and wondered, what could I do?
Then I remembered a piece of card.

So I ran to where I'd seen it,
But all I could see was dust,
So I ran back, but on the way I found this piece of card,
It said to move the rust!

So I went back and moved the rust
And underneath there was a lock,
By it was a message,
The message said *Just Knock!*

So I knocked and knocked,
Then inside I saw treasure,
I cried and cried and then I said,
'I'll be rich forever and ever!'

Catherine Scothern (10)
Kingswood Primary School

RAINBOWS

Red is for anger allied with hate,
Orange is for enjoying things with our best mate,
Yellow is for sunshine sparkling in my eyes,
Green is for plant life of whatever size,
Blue is for sorrow, oceans and seas,
Purple is for your family, for us to please,
Indigo lies deep within the mind
And is for everything on Earth and all mankind.

Melissa Martin-Hughes (10)
Lakeside Primary School

THE KNIGHT

The knight on horseback
was grand as a pea,
Weaving and leaving
like going to sea,
Bumping and jumping
castling high,
Colliding and riding
in the sky.

The knight in guarding
sleeping like a bird,
Roaring and snoring
like elephants in a herd,
Talking and walking
letting folk in,
Muttering and tuttering
big man in a tin.

The knight locking up
all on his own,
Clattering and battering
having a moan,
Smashing and lashing
looking up way so high,
Breaking and shaking
I say what a nice guy.

Becky Waterhouse (9)
Lakeside Primary School

THE BUNGEE-JUMPER

I put on my harness and jump,
Falling like a bird with broken wings,
The secrets of the air, along my shooting path,
On and on I plunge;
Over hunting eagles searching for their prey,
Into cliffs, towering tall and straight every day,
Over clouds which loom like giant balls of cotton wool,
Look, a field with trees and grass,
Vanishes into fog -
I imagined that field . . . what does that mist hold?
Hidden treasure in old wooden barrels,
Lying undisturbed for many years?
The great Tutankhamen, lying mummified in his tomb?
Surrounded by riches, blocks of diamonds, bronze goblets?
I shall never know, too soon the rope sways,
Stops and bounces
And pulls back past the cliffs,
Gently swaying, up I shoot,
To the cliff top, the chattering people,
The ordinary world.

Annie Dickinson (9)
Lakeside Primary School

PIZZA

Pizza comes in different sizes,
Large, medium and small.
There are different toppings with lots of spices,
But I love them all.

My favourite is a thin and crispy,
I think that it's the best.
I reckon that the deep pan must be
The worst in the west.

All the other kinds,
I think are OK.
When it comes to making the choice,
I always have my way.

Amy Higgins (10)
Lakeside Primary School

CAR SICK

I'm in the car
Travelling along
When my stomach
Starts playing a tune

It starts going up and down
And over and over
And round and round
Like a washing machine

I open a window
But not a door
I open a sunroof
And I get a good breeze

I open a drawer
And ask to go home
I pull out a sick bag
And here I go

Belch, belch
Drip, drip
I was sick on my sister
And got hit round the lip!

Elliot Miller (10)
Lakeside Primary School

PARACHUTING

I put on my parachute and jump,
Dropping like an injured bird with attitude,
The secrets of the sky, along my gravestone path,
On and on I glide –
Above swaying trees which with a blow,
Wave like 100 football fans glaring at the ball wherever it goes;
Over chimneys with smoke that makes me vanish,
Look, a family of birds flying north at my side,
Disappears in a flash –
Those birds were swans! . . . Does that cloud hide a fierce storm
Which will come down and make the people praise its nastiness?
Surrounded by soldiers to protect its nastiness,
Is the storm my enemy? I shall never know,
Too soon I hit the ground,
Slowly and painfully,
I try to stand up but my leg hurts,
Slowly, I crawl back to the site,
The noisy aeroplane, the ordinary world.

Vanessa Cotton-Betteridge (10)
Lakeside Primary School

THE SEASONS POEM

The flowers wave, then drift their way on
Swaying and dazing as if the moon is capsizing
Their prettiness and petals among

The sun fires, then brightens on
Blazing and fighting as if a sandstorm is raging
Its sparkle and glistens among

The leaves come pouring, then swiftly move through the air
Twirling and swirling as if the Armada has just come on
Its detail and twigs among

The snow comes dashing, then melts on the ground
Howling and hunting as if a wolf is transforming
Its coldness and whiteness among

The seasons bring so much fun
Tottering, burning, plunging and descending
Their loveliness to always prefer.

Georgina Pugh (9)
Lakeside Primary School

You!

You!
Your eyes are like balls of fire.
You!
Your ears are eager as cats' ears.
You!
Your mind is like a football.
You!
Your body is like a huge boulder.
You!
Your legs are like lightning.
You!
You run like a tiger.
You!
You kick like David Beckham.
You!
You jump like a chimp.
You!
You play like a professional football player.

Cameron Harpin (8)
Mitton Manor Primary School

FRIENDSHIP

Oh great one
I want to be your friend
Forever and ever without a mistake
When the ice burns
And the birds stop singing
When it snows in summer
And when the sun shines in the winter
When the sun and moon turn dull
And the stars fall from the sky
When the flowers die
And monkeys stop swinging
When Dalmatians lose their spots
Not till then will our friendship end.

Robert Jeal (8)
Mitton Manor Primary School

YOU

You!
Your eyes are like a midnight cat!
You!
Your hair is like vines from ivy crawling up a tree!
You!
Your arms are as strong as gravity!
You!
Your legs are as fast as lightning!
You!
Your feet are as big as Jupiter!
   You're the best person ever!

Alex Williams (9)
Mitton Manor Primary School

FRIENDSHIP

O' great one!
I want to be your friend,
Forever and ever without breaking up,
When there's no more chocolate
And the ice cream melts,
When the sun stops shining,
So the moon won't reflect onto Earth,
When the birds die out
And the beasts all starve,
When the last volcano erupts,
With the towns near in rubble,
When the fuel all runs out
And the ozone layer breaks,
When the water doesn't recycle,
So we will become thirsty,
When the world collides with the sun,
Only then will our friendship end.

James Blencowe (8)
Mitton Manor Primary School

BE MY FRIEND

Bonjour,
I want to be your friend,
Forever and ever, I want you to be my friend,
When all the ice creams have all ran out
And even when the sun still shines during the night,
When the birds stop singing,
When all the dogs die out,
When the heavens might open,
Not till this happens I will part from you.

Natalie Potter (8)
Mitton Manor Primary School

You!

You!
Your eyes are small rugby balls.
You!
Your ears are like satellite dishes.
You!
Your mind is as fast as a fired bullet.
You!
Your body is as tough as a steel pole.
You!
Your legs are like a speedy car.
You!
You run like a jaguar.
You!
You throw like a champion.
You!
You dance like a great winner.
You!
You are the best rugby player in the world!

Andrew Mobey (9)
Mitton Manor Primary School

Silver

Your eyes are like silver gleaming.
The sky is silver, the moon is white.
Listen to the birds whistle through the night.
When the street lights are on,
They shine across the river
Like gleaming light.

Tom Moss (8)
Mitton Manor Primary School

YOU!

You!
Your eyes are as big as a panther's.
You!
Your ears are as quick as a running fox.
You!
Your mind is as sharp as a dagger.
You!
Your body is as powerful as a raging buffalo.
You!
Your legs are as strong as a lion.
You!
You run like a cheetah in full sprint.
You!
You jump like a kangaroo.
You!
You throw a ball as high as a house.
You are the best sportsman in the world!

Lauren Castello (8)
Mitton Manor Primary School

HIDDEN TREASURE

Frozen in time lying on a sheep fleece with hoary paws
Claws like thorns embedded in soft paws
Hue of mandarin with peachy stripes splashed over his body
Lustrous sage eyes looking so winsome
A tender tummy, a milky patch up his neck looking supple
Sleek fur like an enormous amber mat.

Chloe Mason (8)
Mitton Manor Primary School

FRIENDSHIP

Oh partner
I want to be your friend
Forever and ever without mistake
When the ice doesn't crack
And the books have no words
When the bacon doesn't sizzle
When the dogs don't bark
And the pencil has no lead
When the leopard has no spots
When the sky has no clouds
And Pluto is hot
When the toast has no butter
When the world is flat
And the skeleton has no bones
When the gun has no bullet
When the birds don't sing
And the clock has no hands
Be my friend, oh please.

Bethan Healy (9)
Mitton Manor Primary School

HIDDEN TREASURE

Gold is rough, gleaming in the sunlight.
Crystals, precious and hiding in the rocks.
Maps are helpful, they tell you where to go.
Friends are friendly, they play with you at school.
Toys are playful, they make you giggle.
Sweets are yummy, you want lots more.

Victor Andrew Howard (8)
Mitton Manor Primary School

FRIENDSHIP FOREVER

Oh partner
I want to be your friend
Forever and ever without any mistakes
When the toast has not cooked and has no butter
When the pop doesn't crackle
And the burgers don't sizzle
When the hedgehogs have no spikes
When the cats don't scratch to get in the house
When the Dalmatians lose their black spots
When the dogs don't bark and howl
When the world is coming to an end
When the storms start coming
And the ice starts to crack
Be my friend, oh partner please.

Jennifer Cromwell (9)
Mitton Manor Primary School

PLEASE BE MY FRIEND

O' great one,
I want to be your friend,
Forever and ever without us parting,
When the deserts are cold
And the freezers are hot,
When the birds stop singing
And the trees run short,
When the world blows
And the planets are pushed back,
When the food runs out of our planet
And no one shall ever argue,
Only then our friendship will part.

Emma Paulson (9)
Mitton Manor Primary School

SEA

The sea, diving around the buoy
The sea, thrashing boats at sea
Crabs scuttling across the shore
The tide driving in down the bay
When the sun sets
The rocks clinging onto the cliff
Sharks lurking by the shore
Fish paddling out in the blue
The waves breaking deep in the blue.

Harry Foster (7)
Mitton Manor Primary School

PRINCESS' POCKET

A golden, magical ring
A bag of jewellery and make-up
A crown with golden jewels
A red ribbon shining in the sun
A posh pair of diamond earrings
Prince Charming waiting for the princess
A pair of shining glass slippers
A bag full of hair clips
An ink pen
A letter from the king.

Emma Williams (7)
Mitton Manor Primary School

FAMILY

My mum is kind to me.
My dad is nice to me.
My sister is jealous of me.
My bird is very noisy.

My dog is playful and lazy.
My nanny is very nice to me.
My cousin is very funny.
All my family are precious to me.

Samantha Danter (8)
Mitton Manor Primary School

NATURE

Waves splashing in the sea.
Rivers running down the mountain.
Snow crunching loudly under my feet.
Current making the river go by.
Children jumping in the sea from high rocks.
Fishes gliding in the pond.
Wind making the sea blow up and down.
Wind blowing soft snow.
Hailstones smashing lots of car windows.

Christopher Williams (7)
Mitton Manor Primary School

CINDERELLA'S POCKET

A glass slipper sparkling
Mice chattering inside the golden pocket
A key glowing
Songs perceptive
A ring with a diamond on
A happy smile
A crown glittering
The prince's love
Stepmother's unkindness
Ugly sisters' bossiness.

Leanne Spry (8)
Mitton Manor Primary School

FOX HUNT

I'm the fox,
I'm the fox.

I lumber through the darkness hunting for my prey,
I pounce on a bird as quick as I can before it flies away.

I'm the fox,
I'm the fox.

I wander through the lanes, you may see my eyes glow,
Or even see my footprints, especially in the snow!

I'm the fox,
I'm the fox.

Here comes the hunter, I'd better run,
Before he has me in his tum!

I'm the fox,
I'm the fox.

I climb over your garden gate
And then I go and fill my plate.

I'm the fox,
I'm the fox.

It's getting light, it's almost dawn,
I fall asleep with one big yawn.

I'm the fox,
I'm the fox,
I'm the fox,
Don't put me in a box!

Katie Cadwallader (9)
Mitton Manor Primary School

NOCTURNAL ANIMALS

Foxes are hunting for some food.
Owls hooting in the moonlight.
Wolves howling through the gloomy wood.
Badgers hibernating through the dark cold winter.
Mice squeaking in the golden cornfields.
Hamsters running round in their wheel.
Bears growling at the midnight moon.

Lizzie Clarke (8)
Mitton Manor Primary School

A FAIRY POCKET

A magic wand
A magic watch
Magic sweets that you can eat forever
A secret diary
A shopping list
A shoe made of crystal
Special magic fairy dust
A sparkling necklace.

Georgina Day (7)
Mitton Manor Primary School

MY FAMILY

Toby is fast and clever.
Mike is funny and intelligent.
Sue is caring and friendly.
Nigel is tough and strong.
Julia is wise and talented.

Oliver Francis (7)
Mitton Manor Primary School

MONSTER'S POCKET!

A dead body looking extremely good,
A piece of moon trying to fool someone,
A tarantula still got all his teeth,
Rocks all smooth and funny shapes,
Some shooting stars blasting in his pocket,
A massive monster tooth, brown and ugly,
A mask making monster look cool,
A weapon to kill somebody,
An alien's phone number to see what the time is,
A space rocket to fly around the world,
A bottle of blood to drink.

Thomas Allcoat (8)
Mitton Manor Primary School

HIDDEN TREASURE!

A lamp shining
A referee's red card
A necklace so sparkly
A colourful lipstick
A golden ring
A chocolate heart
Flowers' aroma
Perfume sweet smelling
A key to a locket
A picture of baby Aladdin
A letter from a genie.

Owen Vincent (7)
Mitton Manor Primary School

ANIMALS

Birds singing to each other on the deep hedgerow
Wolves howling in the dark gloomy wood
Squirrels nibbling at a golden nut tree
Snakes slithering through the green busy grass
Butterflies floating in the fresh blue sky
Kitten miaowing as it was lost in the park
Guinea pigs squeaking on the smooth, colourful, bright carpet
Fish waving its flashing tail under the wavy sea
Kangaroos bouncing in the hot, scorching desert
Spiders crawling up the silver, glistening cobweb
Elephant raising its trunk up the tree to grab some leaves.

Annie Wilkinson (7)
Mitton Manor Primary School

10 THINGS FOUND IN AN ALIEN'S POCKET

Gooey mush that will last forever
People's bodies flowing with blood
Spare eyes in case the others fall out
Funny words in alien
A spaceship flying around
A people disguise for when he goes down to Earth
Stars, the moon and the planets all glowing in the dark
Magic powers, silly ones too
A funny phone where he speaks different languages
Gooey things to eat for lunch.

Laura Griffin (8)
Mitton Manor Primary School

A DRAGON'S POCKET

Some human bodies rotting and turning red
Lots of different bones from everywhere
Millions of horses' heads and fur on fire
Hundreds of hot fires but much hotter than volcano lava
Human armour burnt and rusted
Melted rocks from the galaxy
Ten fat elephants rotten and dead
A whole castle of soldiers all over the world
Fourteen little monsters from Jupiter
Six TVs about dragons v monsters.

Sam Gray (8)
Mitton Manor Primary School

FRIENDS!

Friends, funny
Friends, memories
Friends, special
Friends, caring
Friends, thoughtful
Friends, silly
Friends, groovy
Friends, helpful
Friends, *forever!*

Connor White (7)
Mitton Manor Primary School

SUNLIGHT

Sunlight is like a glowing yellow diamond
reflecting onto fields making them look like
a flowing sea of yellow and green in the wind.

Sunlight is like a sunflower and an angel's smile.

The colour of summer and spring and holiday time.

Sunlight is the god of light, the colour of Heaven.

Giving us light to live forever.

Joe Johnson (11)
North Cerney CE Primary School

MY CAT

As my cat cuddles up into a ball of fur,
I can slightly hear his warming purr.

My cat sits looking all proud and posh,
then suddenly decides to have a wash.

He wiggles his tail as he stalks his toys,
then jumps through the air with barely a noise.

In the bathroom he jumps up to drink from the tap,
then climbs up on my bed to have a long nap.

I love my cat, he's my furry friend,
my love for him will never end.

Kitty Mounstephen (9)
St David's Primary School, Moreton-In-Marsh

HAUNTED CASTLE

Ghosts chased the grey mist
around the tall, black, gloomy castle.
Terrifying, rusty, old skeletons
hung from deep down chambers
like shadows in the dark gloom.
The castle is surrounded by empty
stone graves with not a soul
lying dead in there for years.
People don't even dare touch the
gate of Haunted Castle.

Elizabeth Allen (9)
St David's Primary School, Moreton-In-Marsh

THE MAN FROM PERU

There was a young man of Peru,
Who stuck his head down the loo!
His hair went all curly,
He called it a swirly,
That silly young man of Peru!

Joe Ladbrook (9)
St David's Primary School, Moreton-In-Marsh

MY DOG

He wags his tail like a propeller,
He barks really loudly,
He looks proud like a fella,
But when I leave him, he stands sadly.

When I tell him to 'sit, lie, stay',
He does it straight away,
I love him very much
And when we're close, our hearts can touch.

Sade Peach (9)
St David's Primary School, Moreton-In-Marsh

BIRDS

A chirping bird trying to hide,
A kookaburra singing with pride.

A parrot talking to himself,
A budgie happily on the shelf.

Birds of prey are swooping down
And eagles are the special crown.

Birds are nearly everywhere,
We need to treat them with extra care.

Carl Luker (9)
St David's Primary School, Moreton-In-Marsh

THE SYCAMORE KEY

One second, soaring like a boomerang,
Another, floating like a feather
Next, settling down like a contented cat,
Now, rising once more in windy weather.

Stephanie Ward (10)
St David's Primary School, Moreton-In-Marsh

MY PUPPY

A tail chaser
A hand nibbler
A fun lover
A jumping spring
A rolling bundle of fluff
A warmth, fire lover
A toe eater
A sweet, head-cocker
A heavy sleeper
A food gobbler
A bed lover
A toy player
A treat scoffer
A sniffer
A snuggler
A coal cruncher . . .
But however bad she can be,
She's my puppy called Queenie!

Daisy Perry (9)
St David's Primary School, Moreton-In-Marsh

NOSE-PICKER ROSE

There was a young girl called Rose,
Who couldn't stop picking her nose,
Her fingers turned green like a long runner bean,
So now she uses her toes!

Sophie Wise (9)
St David's Primary School, Moreton-In-Marsh

DOLPHIN

Racing quickly,
He feels quite sickly.

Fin in hand,
We swim over the sand.

Fast he glides, over the sea,
Hand in fin, Scooby and me.

He gives me a ride,
Mother by his side.

Suddenly he sees I'm staring,
Makes a frown, but knows I'm caring.

Samantha Jeffrey (8)
St David's Primary School, Moreton-In-Marsh

SHADOWS

Shadows like to play
with you all day,
they stick to you
like superglue.
Sometimes you wish it would
leave you alone,
but at least they don't moan.
Having a shadow is like
having a best friend,
who will go with you
to the end.

Melissa Day (10)
St David's Primary School, Moreton-In-Marsh

TED

My little sweet teddy called Ted,
I've lost his very soft head,
I've looked high and low,
Even where the flowers grow.
My little sweet teddy called Ted,
My little sweet teddy called Ted,
I've found his very soft head,
He was under my pillow,
He's such a good fellow,
My little sweet teddy called Ted.

Megan Hartnell (8)
St David's Primary School, Moreton-In-Marsh

HIDDEN TREASURE

H iding deep in the darkness of the sea
I nto the depths of deserted places
D ense mist rules over the water
D eep caves are shrouded with colourful coral
E nter a watery world full of mystery
N othing appears to your eyes as it seems

T he battered galleon lies wrecked on ocean floor
R andomly the bones of once-famous pirates scatter the ship's deck
E ach one bleached with the sea's personality
A dark shape flowing through the water
S cavenging for the sea's bounty
U nrestrained in the deep fathoms
R espect the environment
E ven in the darkness of the sea.

Nikolas Powis (11)
St Lawrence Primary School, Lechlade

IT IS MY HIDDEN TREASURE

Somewhere in my memory
Is a special time.
When I went to the seaside,
It really was divine.
It is my hidden treasure.

The journey was quite boring,
I nearly fell asleep.
But the noise was much too loud,
So I started counting sheep.
It is my hidden treasure.

When we finally got there,
To the warm, sandy beach,
The first thing that I did,
Was sit down to eat a peach.
It is my hidden treasure.

I had fun all day,
Playing in the sand
And then, in the evening,
We will listen to a brass band.
It is my hidden treasure.

Finally, time to go home,
I've had a brilliant day.
But now it's time to go to bed
And at home I will stay.
It is my hidden treasure.

Catherine Hope (10)
St Lawrence Primary School, Lechlade

HIDDEN TREASURE

In the dark and haunted room,
Lies beneath the gloom,
Something so sweet,
Lost in a long lost sleep.

Its sweet, fruity scent,
Fills the air behind the fence,
People say the one man who can
Take it in pride and treasure it.

It's time I found my courage,
One step at a time, I rummage through,
I found a box, it looked like my father's,
I looked and in the box I found . . .

It was beautiful, it shined and shined,
Its colour reflected the sun,
Though there was none.

Soon as I picked it up,
The door was no longer shut,
My dad came in,
With a grin.

'What are you doing with my pudding?'

Jenna Kennedy (10)
St Lawrence Primary School, Lechlade

MY HIDDEN TREASURE

I was in the middle of the sea,
I threw my special treasure in,
I watched it sink down, down,
Down into the dark waters,
In till it returned to the golden sand,
Landed with a soft thump.

So I set off home,
By the time I was 80 years old,
Someone discovered my special treasure,
It broke my heart,
Because I wanted it to stay
Under the sea forever,
Or someone to find it when
I had passed away.

Polly New (11)
St Lawrence Primary School, Lechlade

HIDDEN TREASURE

We searched in the pond
We searched far and wide
But all we could find was
A key under the slide

We thought it might be
The key for the chest
But it was the key we kept for the best

We looked in the dog's bowl
We looked under a tree
Nothing we found, not even a pea

Then out of the blue Grandma came running
What genius
What cunning

She had found the key
For the chest
We thought it must be
So we headed west
To the chest to see.

Alastair Blower (11)
St Lawrence Primary School, Lechlade

HIDDEN TREASURES

A carpet of green,
Orange and red,
I swam through the sea
And through the flower bed.

I remember the time,
When I saw fishes swim
Into a cave,
Where the light grew dim.

I went to the cave
And what did I see?
A treasure trove hiding,
Through the debris.

A sparkling ring,
A ruby red,
All these things I could see
In the flower bed.

A multicoloured fish swam past me
And made me think what I should do.
Should I leave this place in peace
Or should I tell the secret to a few?

Katherine Dipple (11)
St Lawrence Primary School, Lechlade

HIDDEN TREASURE

The treasure was buried for a thousand years,
it was not meant to be found.
But when at last the time did come,
the world became drowned,
in one tremendous, vicious fight,
to claim the many riches.

From mouse to elephant,
boy to girl,
from eagles and to finches.
The feelings were bad, the tension was high,
it was very, very hard to decide.
But then after many years,
they came to a decision,
they scooped it up and buried it in a restricted division.

Emma-Louise Pritchard (10)
St Lawrence Primary School, Lechlade

HIDDEN TREASURES

Oh no! I have lost my ring,
Perhaps I will bring
Something better than that,
Like my furry ginger cat!

Grandpa and I,
Will fly in the sky,
But if we crash,
We will not be able to have bangers and mash!

Oh no! I have lost my teddy
And his name is Eddy,
I think I will pack
Some things from my other rucksack!

Grandpa and I,
Will win something from a coconut shy,
We will play bowling
And even go potholing!

Oh no! I have lost my pyjamas,
Because I am sleeping round Grandpa's and Grandma's!

Victoria Button (10)
St Lawrence Primary School, Lechlade

IN MY TREASURE BOX

In my treasure box I'd put,
The first baby's laugh.
The secret of a child's whisper.
The joyful scream of a happy mother.
The deep groan of a father
Who lost a football match.
The sly laugh as the burglar lifts the latch.

In my treasure box I'd put,
The first sighting of a great blue whale.
The last sighting of a dodo.
The look on the faces of people
Who see the crown jewels.
The hurricane I spied.
The man's look as he died.

In my treasure box I'd put,
The touch of a silk sari.
The feel of the fur of a monkey.
The first roar of a lion.
The smell of a beautiful flower
And the scent of power.

Christina Codling (11)
St Lawrence Primary School, Lechlade

HIDDEN TREASURE

Hiding deep, resting in the sands
Waiting to be taken by strong firm hands
In its time of many years
You'd think it would have shed some tears

Until one day rocks started to budge
Out of the cracks came a load of sludge
And as the chest began to drift
The treasure inside began to lift

It found itself on the beach
The sun beaming like a golden peach
Then those hands finally came
It was the chest they came to claim

And its life was ended as it was prised open
Inside was the sparkling token
So the chest's life was over!

Alexandre Duncan (11)
St Lawrence Primary School, Lechlade

HIDDEN TREASURES

Papers advertised 'Treasure galore',
On top of the ceiling, under the floor.
Searching, came with me Auntie Loo,
All my classmates, Grandma and the teacher too.
Where's the treasure? Nowhere!

We searched here, we searched there,
We searched in a cave belonging to a bear.
Over the church steeple,
Looking amongst all the people.
Where's the treasure? Nowhere!

We came to a wood, all dark and scary,
The teacher called out, 'Be very wary.'
We dug over here, we dug over there,
We climbed up trees - that was a dare!
Where's the treasure? Nowhere!

We gave up and decided to go home,
Walking without treasure - all alone.
When I got home I flopped on my bed
And felt something knobbly under my head . . .

Jessica Martin (10)
St Lawrence Primary School, Lechlade

HIDDEN TREASURES

I dreamt one night that I found,
sparkling treasure far below ground.
I went on a journey, under the sea,
I wanted the treasure just for me.

> Legends are told
> about depths deep and cold.
> What traps will there be
> lying hidden for me?

I picked the lock and lifted the lid,
my arms were shaking like a squid.
In that treasure chest, so old,
were many piles of silver and gold.

> I woke to see the orange sun rise,
> with golden coins digging into my sides.
> Silver, glittering pearls in my pocket,
> red rubies, green emeralds and a golden locket.

Isabella Richards (11)
St Lawrence Primary School, Lechlade

HIDDEN TREASURE

Hidden treasure locked away,
Inside a chest of dreams,
But never to be found again,
Till the promise bursts at the seams.

Buried deep, so far, so low
And not to be searched for,
The treasure is so specially hidden,
Continuously making it hurt more.

A hidden treasure such as this,
May never be discovered
And when the time at last will come,
Eventually the secret will be uncovered.

Christina Shields (10)
St Lawrence Primary School, Lechlade

THE HIDDEN SMILE

A sad, old man with a broken heart,
that was created long ago.
Has he ever smiled? Will he ever smile?
Only one person will ever know.
He has memories of love,
with one person only.
The moment she left him,
he knew he'd be lonely.

A creak of door hinges,
a woman steps in.
It was a long time ago,
since she last saw him.
With a tear in the old man's eye,
he remembered goodbye.

A hidden treasure, deep inside,
shows itself for all to see.
A smile. A smile,
oh a glorious smile
and then laughter
and then tears.
Then she left him with a broken heart,
for the rest of his sorrowful years.

Harriet Thomas (10)
St Lawrence Primary School, Lechlade

HIDDEN TREASURE

I sailed on the high blue sea,
looking for treasure for me.
I looked all around,
without a sound,
with a friend called Zee.

We looked in rocks,
we broke some locks.
We swam down,
with a frown,
but found pirate docks.

I played with Zee
in the open sea.
Still looking for the treasure,
we didn't now whether,
to give up or to flee.

We found the treasure,
with ease from a feather.
Me and Zee jumped with joy
and said, 'Oh boy'
then set out to sea.

Chesney Gandhi (10)
St Lawrence Primary School, Lechlade

HIDDEN TREASURES

The dark chest of memories, hidden in my mind,
Some thoughts painful, others happy and fine.
I remember the day, I went to the sea
And saw a strange crab, looking strangely at me.
He drew me towards him, with that silly, strange look
And with his hard claw, my hand he took.
He led me away to a cave in the rock,
Where was a real chest, from inside a knock.

I opened the lid, with a groan and a creak
And inside was a crab, afraid and meek.
Underneath the crab was treasure galore,
It was amazing, exciting, but I didn't want more.
I'd rescued the crab and that was all I wished,
So I left there the chest, for the sea and the fish.
I crept out of my memories, out of my dreams,
I remember those crabs and they'll remember me.

Chloë Nicoll (10)
St Lawrence Primary School, Lechlade

HIDDEN TREASURE

Hidden treasure all around,
anything could be found.
Any age, any time,
but none of it was mine.
Dig and dig,
down and down.
The more you dig, the more you find.

Hidden treasure all round,
anything could be found.
Silver, bronze and gold,
but no one must be told.
More and more,
keeps coming up.
How much more will I find?

Hidden treasure all around,
anything could be found.
The world's wonder,
must be under,
where you stand.

Ruth Howlett (11)
St Lawrence Primary School, Lechlade

HIDDEN TREASURE

My glorious, sparkling treasure,
lies at the bottom of the sea.
The creatures swim around it,
looking up at me.

I dive down in my submarine
and have a look around.
When suddenly it came at me,
a slimy, big, black, ugly mound.

I turned around and drove away,
not daring to look back.
When suddenly I realised I was on an oil tank,
which took me straight to land.

From that day, I never forgot,
the big, black, ugly mound,
that guards my treasure,
forever.

Tom Traas (10)
St Lawrence Primary School, Lechlade

HIDDEN TREASURE

Hidden treasure lost and found,
Sparkling gold under the ground.
Only I knew about this wonder,
Digging quickly, under, under.

I found the map in an ancient book,
I looked at it and then took.
Took it to where the 'X' was drawn,
Then my adventure was newly born.

Now I stare down at the wooden chest,
Wondering if I should leave it to rest.
They say being rich can have an effect,
So I buried it back and quickly left.

Katy Brewer (10)
St Lawrence Primary School, Lechlade

HIDDEN TREASURES

My dad made a submarine
It was yellow and bright green
He said that I could go in it
Me, my dog and Grandad Kit

We all got in and turned the key
Then we were gliding through the sea
We saw some fish wriggle past
The creatures were a lovely cast

The ship made a whistle and a bark
At the sight of a great white shark
Then - I spotted a glowing box
In-between the coloured rocks

The ship magically picked it up
We looked out the window and even the pup
We started going back to land
To the sky and to the golden sand

Because my dad made a submarine
Painted yellow and bright green
We found some treasure under the sea
And we're all happy and full of glee.

Lucinda Popp (11)
St Lawrence Primary School, Lechlade

HIDDEN TREASURE

She jumped off the ship and splashed,
Then fell down and her air tank bashed,
On a wooden chest bordered in gold,
It was beautiful but very old,
Covered in seaweed and sand,
I don't think anyone could open it by hand,
Guarded by fish and a shark,
Under the sea it was very dark,
She tried to open it and it worked,
It opened and there was a fish perched on gold,
Which was never meant to be sold,
There were crowns, jewellery and pearls
And it matched with her golden curls,
She brought it up to the land,
Because she was running out of air,
But she had trapped her hand,
Now it was free but as she got to the top,
The treasure slipped out of her hands
Back into the sea where it should be.

Tia Gammond (10)
St Lawrence Primary School, Lechlade

HIDDEN TREASURES

The old, rugged chest lies there in the sand,
I looked in the sea to see my own hand.
It's right by the rocks, lies there in the dark,
Safe from the pirates or even a shark.

Who knows what's inside the dark chest,
People try but never rest.
The children wonder who is best,
To have the diamond on their chest.

We found the treasure loud and clear,
Then I said, 'Oh, it's queer.'
We opened the chest to see what was in,
Then we saw a diamond, clean and thin.

We couldn't believe it, what a sight,
There it lay, sparkling bright.
We put the diamond in a tin,
Then went to the sea and threw it back in.

Jack Marston (10)
St Lawrence Primary School, Lechlade

HIDDEN TREASURE

Deep down under the sea,
A fish was drinking tea,
It swam to the bottom of the ocean,
As if it was under a magical potion.

Through a hole in a ship, it happily went
And into the hole as if mysteriously sent.
Something was shining as the fish simply said,
'That's much too shiny to be someone's head.'

So the fish went to see, just what this could be,
It might be real treasure,
To be gathered at leisure.

He swam to the shore,
He wanted to see things he hadn't seen before,
But when he got there,
The chest was bare.

Captain Saunders had already been.

Stephanie Dyos (11)
St Lawrence Primary School, Lechlade

HIDDEN TREASURE

I'm all alone,
On my own,
Striding down the beach,
For I need to reach
The hidden treasure,
That is within my measure,
The soul inside
Had been washed aside,
Onto the silky sand,
That I will touch with my hand,
The power inside full of belief,
Or maybe even grief.

Oh what is this, I have found?
This is it, lying on the ground,
I slowly touched it
And then I felt fit,
I suddenly felt an urge to drink mud,
No, no, this taste was blood!
Suddenly I felt myself transform,
My soul inside had been torn,
I grew some wings,
Tiny things,
Oh look, I am a bat,
A very fat bat.

I soared up into the sky,
Oh my, oh my, oh my!
My teeth are sharp and long
And give off a pong,
Then it hit me,
I had lost my taste for tea,
I am a vampire,
I have received the soul inside,
The treasure washed aside,

I am the founder of the treasure
So I know the soul inside
It is a vampire's soul
Ahhhh!
Now the spirit is all alone,
All on his own.

Thomas Massey (11)
St Lawrence Primary School, Lechlade

LOVE

Deep down in my memory,
I remember a time when I found love.
Sweet, sweet love like never before,
I've always dreamt of it,
Now my dreams come true.

I finally found my destination,
In my lover's arms.
He bears me gifts of golden rings
And love is forever in my heart,
For him who loves me so.
I will always remember the time,
When we first met with love at first sight.
Deep down in my memory,
I remember a time when I found love.

Lizzy Reeves (10)
St Lawrence Primary School, Lechlade

MY DRAGON

My dragon is nice
My dragon has head lice
My dragon is tame
My dragon is lame
My dragon is funny
My dragon likes bunnies
My dragon keeps rats
My dragon eats cats
My dragon is fond of cakes
My dragon drinks cornflakes
My dragon does think
But . . .
My dragon is the weakest link!

Billie Arnold (9)
St Paul's CE Primary School, Gloucester

SPORTS DAY

The sports day run
Is extremely fun

The sports day jump
Everybody goes thump!

The sports day throw
The balls says go, go, go

The sports day walk
No time to talk

Sports day has ended
It's not totally what I recommended.

Connor Gwilliam (8)
St Paul's CE Primary School, Gloucester

DOLPHINS

D   olphins jumping up and down making their cheerful dolphin sound.
O   ver, across the big blue sea, I see dolphins squealing with glee.
L   eaping dolphins in the air splashing back down in despair.
P   rancing and dancing round and round, making their cheerful
                                  dolphin sound.
H   appy sleeping in their home, no one to wake them all alone.
I   n the water dolphins glide, going fast like a slide.
N   ot a single person has disturbed them.
S   o now be quiet as the dolphins go to sleep, sh, sh!

Katy Hogan (9)
St Paul's CE Primary School, Gloucester

MY COLOURS

Blue is the sky colour,
Yellow is the sun's colour,
Green is the grass colour,
Pink is my skin colour,
Red is a strawberry's colour,
Orange is an orange's colour,
Purple is the flower's colour.

Blue,
Yellow,
Green,
Pink,
Red,
Orange,
Purple
Are my favourite colours.

Ria Meredith (9)
St Paul's CE Primary School, Gloucester

MY PET CAT

My pet cat is plain weird,
he headbutts everything in sight,
he gives my mum a fright.

He fights and he bites,
but these terrible things
he doesn't count . . .
because he was born this way,
that's all.

Other cats are peaceful,
but he's a maniac!
As I sleep, he's sick
with a *squeak.*

He's just plain weird,
but he's my cat.

Adam Davis (9)
St Paul's CE Primary School, Gloucester

DOLPHINS

D   olphins swimming a synchronised dance.
O   ceans where they love to play.
L   oud and noisy playing swimming tag.
P   recious friends forever.
H   iding and seeking wherever they go.
I   ntruding in other people's games.
N   ever ever hurt anyone.
S   aying sorry wherever they go.

Nicola Bishop (8)
St Paul's CE Primary School, Gloucester

I HAVE A GRANDAD

I have a grandad,
He was in the army
And he was a plumber.

I have a grandad,
He was a swimming teacher
And a therapist.

I have a grandad,
My grandad had a son
And his son had me!

I have two grandads,
They're very nice to me,
One is very, very funny
And the other is full of glee.

Katherine Randall (8)
St Paul's CE Primary School, Gloucester

ROLLER COASTER

Roller coasters in the air,
whizzing up and down.
Some blue, some red,
different sizes, big and small.
Looping down the track,
going clickety clack.
Along the track,
with people screaming.
To the roller coasters,
stop!

Adam Stanton-Lee (8)
St Paul's CE Primary School, Gloucester

IF THERE WAS A SPACE

If there was a space,
I would fly to the moon,
I'd tell everyone,
There wasn't much room.

If there was a space,
I would fly to Pluto,
I'd tell everyone,
Please do so.

If there was a space,
I would fly to Saturn,
I'd tell everyone,
There is a pattern.

If there was a space,
I would fly to Mars,
I'd tell everyone,
They do chocolate bars.

Emma Mathieson (8)
St Paul's CE Primary School, Gloucester

MY BIG DOG

My big dog is really lazy.
My big dog is very fat.
He is white with big black spots.
He dozes by the blazing fire
And whenever it's dinner time,
He zooms into the kitchen
And when he finishes,
He waddles back to the blazing-hot fireplace.

Alec Nisbet (8)
St Paul's CE Primary School, Gloucester

DOLPHINS

D eep in the blue sea, dolphins swim gracefully in peace!
O n the world above they jump so high in the sky, just for fun!
L eap so high it makes you cry! Don't worry it won't hurt!
P lease don't cry, they might go away! Sniff! Sniff!
H urt you they won't, so leave them alone! Please!
I f you see them hurt! Take care of them.
N eed them or not, they are such fun!
S wimming with them is such fun!

Khadijah Pandor (8)
St Paul's CE Primary School, Gloucester

SWIMMING

S wimming is so fun.
W ater splashing in your face.
I n the swimming pool more water, it gets higher.
M any more children go and play around.
M um likes going, she likes getting her hair wet.
I n I go, in the pool, I splash, wandering about.
N asty taste has the water.
G o on in, says my mum.

Louie Reid (8)
St Paul's CE Primary School, Gloucester

MY CAT

My cat is snuggly, buggly and cute.
He likes to fight with the dog
And roam the streets at night.
But I guess that's what cats do!

Frances Jane Coleman (8)
St Paul's CE Primary School, Gloucester

EGYPT

E gyptians are like diamonds, glittering all night.
G od sent the message through Egypt.
Y et there's more information to come.
P haraohs nicely mummified.
T utankhamen twirling and twisting.

Ashley Barnby (9)
St Paul's CE Primary School, Gloucester

WHAT IF THE QUEEN'S SKIRT FELL DOWN?

What if the Queen's skirt fell down?
I think she'd run away,
She'd run away until she's in town
And there I think she'd stay.

What if the Queen's skirt fell down,
In the middle of her Jubilee?
She'd knock on my door, in the town
And ask to stay for tea.

What if the Queen's skirt fell down,
Opening a store?
She'd never have a frown, upside down
And would run straight for the door.

What if the Queen's skirt fell down,
Whilst reading to the poor?
She would run out of the town
And lock all of the doors.

What if the Queen's skirt fell down?
Of course it could never be,
She would never wear a frown,
Like she won't spill her tea.

Toni Andrea Smith (10)
Siddington CE Primary School

138

FAIRIES

I believe in fairies
They fly around all day
I believe in fairies
But some may say they don't
I believe in fairies
And it will always stay that way.

Kathryn Morgan (10)
Siddington CE Primary School

GUESS WHO?

Works on cars
Eats chocolate bars
Snores in bed
Roll out of bed
It will be
My dad.

Alex Hicks (9)
Siddington CE Primary School

PENGUINS IN THE ZOO

Penguins playing in their pool
Eating fish and wanting more
Playing with their ball, they look so cool,
Diving in the water, two foot deep, like the divers in the deep.

Matthew Gardner (10)
Siddington CE Primary School

MONSTERS

The bogeyman comes from under your bed
and puts little boogies under your head.

The sandman comes from the sky
and puts bits of sand in your eye.

Now here is a list of the monsters you'll find,
if you go to a cupboard then look behind:

One-eyed demons with sharp claws,
man-eating plants with horrid jaws.

Poisonous slugs and dreadful gnomes
and furry beasts chewing large bones.

So if you're looking for a scare,
the first place you must go is there.

Boo!

Amber Jane Stranks (10)
Siddington CE Primary School

UNTITLED

Book reader,
Dart player,
Bingo winner,
Child lover,
Tea maker,
EastEnders watcher,
Mess hater,
That's my mother!

Danielle Linda Walker (10)
Siddington CE Primary School

THE CLASS

Lots of work,
Big smirk.

Open windows,
Big crescendos.

Pencils, pens,
No hens.

Chairs and tables,
Lots of cables.

Pencil cases,
Shoes and laces.

Metal, brass,
My class!

Jake Addison Hogan (10)
Siddington CE Primary School

GUESS WHO?

Brilliant cooker
Keen gardener
Best housekeeper
Dinner maker
Child lover
Coffee drinker
Ironing hater
Candle collector
Ornament liker
Great decorator
Loud shouter

My mother.

Zoë Cook (11)
Siddington CE Primary School

TAKEAWAY DINNER WITH THE QUEEN

The Queen is coming to dinner tonight!
What a scare! What a fright!
I wonder what the Queen will say,
When I bring the takeaway?

The Queen will come in her satin gown,
Also in her shiny crown.
But I wonder how she will feel,
When she sees our junky meal?

I really hope that the Queen
Doesn't order strawberries and cream
And I hope she will be happy enough,
With all this very greasy stuff.

Elliot Cass (11)
Siddington CE Primary School

MY HIDDEN TREASURES

H   ippos like to swim in dirty rivers
I   f I swam in them, I'd get the shivers
D   olphins like to dance in the sea
D   eer like to prance beside me
E   lephants are grey and tall
N   ewts are scaly and small

T   igers are cats with stripes of black
R   hinos have horns and armour on their back
E   agles soar up high in the sky
A   nts work harder than you and I
S   harks' teeth are sharper than a knife
U   nicorns don't exist in real life
R   ats are rodents that carry germs
E   els are long and wriggly like giant worms
S   o that's all about the animal life.

Elena Finch (9)
Swindon Village Primary School

HIDDEN TREASURES

H ilarious fish breathing extremely slow,
I cy oceans is what the sea lions love,
D ancing dolphins swimming marvellously,
D ogfish remind me of my playful dog, Ben,
E agle rays swimming swiftly along the ocean bed,
N aughty Napoleon wrasses eating loads of fish.

T iger fish have beautiful colours but have deadly poison,
R ainbowfish swimming with their friends,
E normous eels pop up at any time,
A ngelfish brightly coloured, many different types,
S ea lions, shiny, black,
U pside-down crocodile fish, they must be crazy!
R acing sharks waiting for their tea,
E nchanting sea horses camouflaged in corals,
S harks basking, frozen to the spot.

Joanna Bundy (9)
Swindon Village Primary School

ANIMALS

H ippos in the squidgy mud, the
I deal place to play
D ancing
D olphins playing ball
E legant eagles flying high in the sky
N aughty octopus

T aking all the fish
R acing rats in a cage
E vil emus pecking people's fingers
A nnoying snakes hissing hour by hour
S ea horses prancing underwater
U nusual hamsters doing
R oly-polys in their cage
E lephants flapping their ears, warning to stay away
S illy humans standing there, oh no they're going to charge!

Samantha Connell (9)
Swindon Village Primary School

HIDDEN TREASURES

H ummingbirds dancing in the air
I guanas sticking up their hair
D olphins doing their tricks
D affy duck playing with his chicks
E lephants stomping on the grass
N earby is a tall giraffe

T igers chasing zebras fast
R abbits running like you're flying past
E lephants eating your grass
A nts walking in a line
S potty dogs out for a walk
U nicorns with their big horns
R attlesnakes slithering through the grass
E lephants are stomping past
S lithering slug, slithering along.

Sam Carter (8)
Swindon Village Primary School

ANIMALS

H iding hounds in the breeze
I guanas drop with a freeze
D onkeys thumping in their stables
D olphins with their shiny labels
E lephants stomping on the grass
N aughty roosters trying to brass

T usks lying on the floor
R unning monkeys trying to score
E agles flapping in the air
A ngry apes doing their stare
S nakes slithering up a tree
U h oh, there's a flea
R abbits running round a tower
E ager chickens having a shower
S h sounds, what's that I hear?

Daniel Griffiths (9)
Swindon Village Primary School

MY HIDDEN TREASURES

H iding
I n the sea
D ancing
D olphins
E nergy
N eeding new

T erritory
R ays
E xploring
A nd
S wimming through a shipwrecked door
U gly crocs, they're best by far
R oaring and
E ating
S ea lions, ahh!

Milli Cornock (9)
Swindon Village Primary School

TOTALLY BONKERS

H airy bear
I ncredibly fair
D angerous Dan
D rives in Afghanistan
E legant cat
N ever eats fat

T iny Tom
R ough and careless
E ggy Ellie
A nd her friend's belly
S limy slug
U gly and smelly
R eckless Rob
E ager to start work
S limy Sam lives in a baker's van.

Matthew Adair (9)
Swindon Village Primary School

NICK'S FREEDOM POEM

When I'm 18 I'm going to be free
I want to be a footballer like Thierry Henry

When I'm 18 I'm going to be free
I want to be a mad rapper like Ali G

When I'm 18 I'm going to be free
I want to tell jokes just like Jack Dee

When I'm 18 I'm going to be free
I want to bowl a cricket ball as fast as Brett Lee

When I'm 18 I'm going to be free
And get away from my family

But I'm only 8 and still waiting at the gate.

Nicholas Mandella (8)
Swindon Village Primary School

ANIMALS

H   amster running
I   n his wheel
D   elightful
D   ogs
E   agles flying in the sky at
N   ight

T   igers
R   oaring so loud
E   lephants
A   sking for love
S   nake hissing
U   nder a log
R   hino that roams freely
E   lephants and all animals living
S   afely forever.

Kelsey Lonergan (8)
Swindon Village Primary School

HIDDEN TREASURES

H idden in the deep
I n the shark-infested sea
D own we go
D olphins peer
E legant whales
N aughty fish

T rying to guard hidden treasures!
R ound and round the sea
E agles fly on top
A nts don't live there
S lithering water snakes
U nder the surface
R ound fish, flat fish
E nchanted sea life
S wim by the hidden treasures!

Tanya Hopson (8)
Swindon Village Primary School

HAPPY PARTIES

H appy parties
I cing on the cake
D ance
D ecide what to do
E at
N ow it's time to eat the cake

T ake off the icing
R ound and round, sing happy birthday
E at the marzipan
A nd then the sponge
S tay sat at the table
U ntil the rest are ready
R un up and collect your goodie bag
E veryone is leaving now
S ay goodbye!

George Ford (8)
Swindon Village Primary School

HIDDEN TREASURES

H ippos running very fast
I guana's tongue is going past
D olphins jumping very high
D ogs are reaching for the sky
E agles are flying, looking good
N ewts with their long tails

T arantulas are dangerous
R hinos charging like a bull
E lephants' minds are very full
A te some nuts, the squirrel has
S nails are listening to jazz
U nder the floorboard at a disco
R ats are dancing at San Francisco
E nding the party the monkey will!
S illy hamsters on their wheel.

Nathan Roberts (8)
Swindon Village Primary School

ANIMALS

H umming, dancing in the air
I guanas sticking up their hair
D izzy dolphins dancing in the sea
D affy duck eating his tea
E agles flying up in the sky
N esting in a tree

T igger chasing toucans all day
R unning rhinos storming this way
E lephants eating grass
A nts lining up on an apple
S lug sliding under leaves
U nicorn riding about
R attlesnake slithering up a tree
E lephant swimming near to me
S pider makes its web.

Jack Stanley (8)
Swindon Village Primary School

ANIMALS

H amster running
I n his wheel
D og chewing its
D elicious bone
E lephants
N ursing their babies

T oads
R unning and hopping fast
E agles flying through the sky
A dders
S lithering on the ground
U nicorns galloping
R ound and round
E lephants love you
S o much.

Danielle Blackwell (8)
Swindon Village Primary School

SUPERSTARS

H enry scores
I nternational star
D azzling
D efender L Thuram who plays for Parma
E ager midfielder Zinedine Zindane
N igerian players

T ottenham hungry for the cup
R aces for The Premiership
E dgar Davids scores, goal, goal, goal
A rsenal players
S cores
U nusual Keown, he looks weird
R angers strikers
E dgar David's just
S cored.

Daniel Kettlety (8)
Swindon Village Primary School

UNTITLED

H oly man that's Steve Book
I cing to the rescue
D odgy striker takes the shot
D idn't you see him miss
E nding the first half, the score is one-
N il

T rying very hard, they get another goal
R ocking the match
E llington hits the post
A way we are at Bristol Rovers
S winging to our tenth win
U know who it is, Tony Nalor
R oaring with excitement
E llington has another chance
S teve Book's on the way to save!

Dale Goodwin (8)
Swindon Village Primary School

ANIMALS

H awks slowly glide through the air
I guanas with their sticky tongues
D ingos jumping through the flames
D olphins in deep water
E lephants bunched tightly, grazing and eating
N ursing their babies with hugs

T igers pouncing and running after prey
R hinos running, single file
E agles eating like vultures
A nts avoiding the crunch
S nakes slithering snail-like trails
U should try to be one
R apidly all the animals go
E yes of the ostrich, big and bulgy
S ee you at my zoo.

Jay Privett (8)
Swindon Village Primary School

HIDDEN TREASURES

H aving a day off school
I 'd like to see my budgie again
D elight in my sister's hamster
D oe a rabbit, my mum's rabbit
E very one of my goldfish
N ice to play on my PlayStation all day

T o see my dog
R unning again
E ven I want to see my nan again
A nd to play on my Game Boy all day
S o all these are special
U have things that are special, so what are they?
R they to
E nd a football win or
S wim with sharks?

Josh Locke (8)
Swindon Village Primary School

HIDDEN TREASURES

H elping others
I s feeling good,
D own in the park,
D ancing with my friends,
E ven chipmunks are a bit
N utty.

T o see my two guinea pigs and my
R abbit again,
E gg and chips
A nd
S ugar are the best!
U mbrellas are good for
R ain and
E ven inside for making dens,
S ome of my hidden treasures are special thoughts.

Katie Dewar (9)
Swindon Village Primary School

HIDDEN TREASURES

My hidden treasures are
my special thoughts.

H igh flying,
I rish dancing,
D ancing fairies,
D riving cars,
E ating food,
N ice friends.

T iddly babies,
R eplaying happy moments,
E ating loads more,
A t home where there are hugs,
S wimming with mermaids,
U niform at school,
R eally wishing to be a popstar,
E ating more food,
S taring up into the sky.

Alice Faith Hooper (8)
Swindon Village Primary School

HIDDEN TREASURES

My hidden treasures are my special thoughts.

H idden treasures under the sea
I get a dog just for me
D ancing dolphins in the ocean
D odging elephants in a football game
E njoying tigers with one name
N ever sad to play a game

T o be a pirate, to fight a war
R acing in a racing car
E lephants dancing with joy
A nimals at a party
S pace, to meet an alien in the scary place
U nhappy - never ever
R ushing to meet my mum
E very day I see my family
S ome of my wishes.

Charlotte McAlary (8)
Swindon Village Primary School

HIDDEN TREASURES

My hidden treasures are my special thoughts.

H appy families make me cheerful,
I njured people make me tearful,
D ead animals make me sad,
D elightful animals make me glad,
E nding wars makes me happy,
N ectarine skins are all flappy.

T oo many injured people on our land,
R uined buildings on the ground,
E ven a little food would fill the hungry up,
A t the bottom, to the top,
S uffering children round the world,
U nderground all curled,
R escue these children,
E ven try because these children are doomed to die,
S o please, please try.

Paige Simic (9)
Swindon Village Primary School

HIDDEN TREASURES

My hidden treasures are my special thoughts.

H igh flying
I n the sky
D isco dancing
D olphins jumping up high
E ating cake, yum, yum
N ice hugs from my mum

T reasures in the garden
R eplaying a good moment
E ating even more cake
A t home where I like it most
S tarting up a brand new car
U sing it to go round the Earth
R evving it up again and again
E ating cake, I want more
S ee Ron Weasley – that's what I'd like the most.

Amy Wright (9)
Swindon Village Primary School

HIDDEN TREASURES

My hidden treasures are my special thoughts.

H igh speed motor cars driving at a cool amount of speed,
I t's a dual carriageway,
D idn't win the race,
D on't mind losing or winning,
E nd of match,
N othing much.

T umbling down a mountain,
R ocks tumbling,
E lephants thumping along,
A girl's room,
S ome people like lollies,
U are good,
R eplay me,
E verybody says hello,
S ick person feeling better.

Simon Williams (8)
Swindon Village Primary School

HIDDEN TREASURES

My hidden treasures are my special thoughts.

H elping others I like best
I t makes me happy
D ancing dolphins
D o make me happy
E ven if they talk to me
N ever ever be scared

T o not walk away from people – let's talk
R iding horses on my own
E ven if I fall off once
A t last someone helped me when I had a broken wrist
S till like horses
U nicorns are like horses but with one horn
R eally do they exist?
E ven better, who knows
S o I like everything.

Briony Watling (8)
Swindon Village Primary School

HIDDEN TREASURES

My hidden treasures are my special thoughts.

H appy days made in Heaven,
I want to be with S Club 7,
D octors and nurses helping out,
D olphins – hear them shout,
E veryone is glad,
N ever sad.

T o cuddle with my old bear,
R oom's full of people who care,
E lephants being bathed – surely they cried?
A nother wish – no one has lied,
S un at the seaside,
U ltra fun,
R un, run, run,
E veryone being good friends,
S ome of my hidden treasures.

Tamara Morgan (9)
Swindon Village Primary School

HIDDEN TREASURES

My hidden treasures are my special thoughts.

H elping animals in need
I njured things upsets me
D olphins - set them free
D ogs licking me
E lephants riding
N esting in a broken tree

T o be a professional violinist
R unning a rescue centre
E ffort in my work
A nimal helping
S haring with the poor
U nknown
R escuing helps others
E ndangered animals kept in zoos to be bred
S nakes having fun on slides.

Emily Pagel (8)
Swindon Village Primary School

HIDDEN TREASURES

My hidden treasures are my special thoughts.

H amsters crawling
I cing on every cake
D ogs licking
D olphins dancing
E rik being kind
N uts for young people

T o see my old dog again
R espect for the poor
E lephants being bathed by me
A pples growing on trees
S easide splashing
U nkind people being kind
R are being looked after
E lephants being treated kindly
S peaking to other people and not walking away.

Anna Hughes (8)
Swindon Village Primary School

HIDDEN TREASURES

My hidden treasures are my special thoughts.

H elping the poor
I s what we need to do
D oing all we can
D o I wish I could help them?
E ven for a year
N ot for two

T he poor need help
R ead to them
E ven sing to them
A nd cook dinner for them
S o help the poor
U ntil you're old
R eturn home
E nd of your travelling
S ure your family will be glad.

Joe Townsend (8)
Swindon Village Primary School

HIDDEN TREASURES

My hidden treasures are my special thoughts.

H elping the poor
I s what you need to do
D on't please things for yourself
D on't be stupid
E ven if you feel like it
N aughty children will copy you

T oo many people die
R uined lives and buildings
E nd the war
A nd live in peace
S urely you help the poor
U se no more guns
R est of the world should be like us
E ven the poor
S o are you?

Peter Griffiths (8)
Swindon Village Primary School

HIDDEN TREASURES

My hidden treasures are my special thoughts.

H appy birthdays
I cing on the cake
D iving
D eep in the sea
E ating Nik Naks
N ice 'n' spicy

T rying to swing from tree to tree
R acing a real chimpanzee
E vergreen
A pples
S tation
U nderground
R oots I like to pull
E ntertaining
S hops, that's for me.

Richard Elsworthy (9)
Swindon Village Primary School

My Hidden Treasures Are My Special Thoughts

H appiness in the world
I would like to be the 8th member of S Club 7
D iving with
D olphins
E den is the place where I want to be
N ibbling marzipan

T eaching and playing with babies
R abbits make me cheerful
E gg and cheese is so nice
A pples being nibbled
S wimming under the sun
U nder the ocean I go
R iding a motorbike
E lephant riding
S wimming in the deep blue sea.

Sian Beames (8)
Swindon Village Primary School

Hidden Treasures

H anging out with my friends,
I deas are great,
D oing art is fun,
D own in the dumps – they make me cheerful,
E lephants are cute,
N ot going to school.

T V all day,
R hyming words together,
E verything will make me happy,
A eroplanes flying high up in the sky,
S aucer scaring people off,
U nhappy people – I make them happy,
R escuing people makes me proud,
E veryone is king,
S inging birds make me happy.

Charlotte Turville (8)
Swindon Village Primary School

My Hidden Treasures Are My Special Thoughts

H elping others
I cing on a cake
D ogs and
D olphins
E lephants
N ice animals roam the Earth

T igers
R un and kill them
E lectric eels
A pples to eat
S ee David Beckham
U nited are the best
R un a race
E ven a mile
S ee my dog, Tyler.

Mathew Farrand (8)
Swindon Village Primary School

The Swan

Flying like a ballerina,
Dancing in the clouds,
As white as snow, so clean,
Though making silent sounds,
Prancing by the meadows,
Skimming through the streams,
Soaring over mountain tops,
Please come back to me.

Connie Langdon (9)
Temple Guiting School

161

THE BEACH

The day has broken,
The people are woken,
The gulls are singing,
The clocks are ringing.
Beaches are quiet,
Ready for the morning riot,
Buckets are picked up,
The parents quickly get a cup.
Beaches are covered with noise once again,
Choc ices are eaten there and then,
Deckchairs are snapped open, ready for an unlucky person,
People get changed behind a curtain,
The waves gallop like white horses,
People live in tents for survival courses,
Will the excitement ever end?
Yes,
The sun is going down, the tide goes out
And it's peaceful once again.

Myles Charles-Jones (10)
Temple Guiting School

DAFFODILS

I wandered lonely as a drunk
That wobbles on high o'er vales and sings
When all at once I saw a punk
With a hoot of long spiky things;
Beside the lake, beneath the sun,
Fluttering and dancing (having fun).

James Macklin (10)
Temple Guiting School

THE OAK TREE

The mighty oak stands tall and proud, swaying in the breeze,
It looks upon the ground below thinking
And as it thinks, it dreams of the rainforest.

Now and again a bird goes and tells the oak what's happening,
The bird tells the oak of amazing tales, flying above the clouds
And the oak stands solidly and listens.

The bird flies here and there from place to place
And tells the other birds he meets to go and talk to the oak,
A day goes by, no visit for the oak, but then,
A flock of birds the oak tree sees, the visit of its dreams.

A party started soon enough, music and the lot
And the oak tree stood and swayed to the music,
Whilst the bird smiled.

Emily Seal (10)
Temple Guiting School

LEPRECHAUN LIMERICKS

A leprechaun called Mike
He rode a motorbike
One day he crashed
His arm got smashed
And now he has to hike!

A leprechaun called Pete
With large and clumsy feet
Fell over Mike
Smashed his teeth on the bike
But the braces are nice and neat!

Matthew East (11)
Temple Guiting School

MOPPET

I have a cat called Moppet,
Who is very mad indeed.
You'll never find a cat like her,
Or another breed.

She chases after rolling pencils
And wobbling bits of string.
She chews it up and bites it hard,
Till it looks like something the cat's brought in (literally!)

She likes to be tickled under her chin
And on top of her head.
She mainly sleeps all of the day,
Curled up on my bed.

I have a cat called Moppet,
Who is very mad indeed.
I wouldn't change her for the world,
'Cause I love her and she loves me!

Katharine Clissold (11)
Temple Guiting School

IF I WAS ...

If I was a dog, I would love my bone.
If I was a footballer, I would hate getting smacked.
If I was a calculator, I would hate to do all the sums.
If I was a cool person, I would love to dance!
If I was a sheep, I wouldn't like the cold.
If I was a rabbit, I would hate to get eaten by a fox.
If I was a cricket bat, I would hate to hurt the ball.
But if I was a rich person, I would share my fortune
With my family and friends.

Ben Hughes (10)
Temple Guiting School

MY SHETLAND

My Shetland is the best
She gallops like a cheetah
And as cuddly as a bear
She sometimes gets frightened
Of things that are as big as a monster

I love my Shetland very much
But sometimes she has to go away
I miss her very much when she goes away
But she will still love me
Wherever she goes

I love my Shetland
And I will never sell her
Because I know that we will be best friends
And we will travel together.

Rebecca Jackson (10)
Temple Guiting School

LIPPIZANER

Milk-white they turn as they get much older
From warm brown and black, their colours get colder

Their glossy mane like silver silk
Their coat as sleek and white like milk

Dancing and bounding like a ballerina
The foals running and jumping in grass much greener

Their glistening eye
As they glide close by.

Camilla Lee-Warner (9)
Temple Guiting School

THE EVIL RED PEN

The English book is opened,
The girl reaches for her pen,
The book breathes in anticipation,
For the girl to start to write,
The pointed nib tickles,
But there is more to come,
For later on, the teacher will,
With her evil red pen,
Come and write her comment,
Criticism and all,
The poor book knows what is waiting to come,
To scratch and stab and cut,
The evil red pen will rise again
And torture the innocent books.

Charlotte Chudleigh (10)
Temple Guiting School

THE NEW CLASSROOM

There's a new classroom being built
And it's a disaster.
The builders are sick.
The dumper truck's broken down.
The digger has crashed.
The cement is leaking.
The toilets have blown over.
The builders' caravan has blown away
And the classroom is not being built.

Toby Harris (11)
Temple Guiting School

166

GALLOPING PONY

I put my saddle on my pony,
Then my bridle.
We set off as the chilly wind starts to blow.
As we set down the village, I am glad I have layers underneath.
Winks was glad too, to have his exercise sheet tucked underneath
his saddle.

A chilly wind went down my spine,
But I knew I was safe in the morning.
In the afternoon, light or sunset,
I turned left as it got a bit lighter.
I jumped off to open the gate,
I got back on again.
I cantered on the wide bridle path,
The other ponies stared at us.
I had to stop again, to open the other gate,
We went through the woodland,
Going steady, just in case
A woodland creature jumped out in front of us.

Isabelle Mangan (9)
Temple Guiting School

DAFFODILS

I wandered lonely as a fly,
That flies around on high o'er vale and hills.
When all at once I saw it flutter by,
A host of a fish that jumped up in the air with golden gills.
Beside the lake I sat looking at the trees,
Fluttering and dancing in the breeze.

Natasha Dutson (9)
Temple Guiting School

SEASONS

First comes *winter* where the first snow falls
While everyone is inside opening presents from
Underneath the Christmas tree
Turkey cooking in the oven, ready for dinner
People going on long snowy walks
Decorations coming down soon, ready for the New Year

Now comes *spring*, when lambs are born
Just in time for the New Year
All the flowers start to grow, daffodils, daisies, tulips and crocus
All the children playing in fields and picking flowers
People start to get ready for their holidays
Or going away with school

Now it's *summer* and everyone in gardens
And playing at friends' catching butterflies
And keep as pets for a while
Everyone at home for their summer holidays
And starting to go on holidays
People going on walks, having fun
People going on bikes, having a massive bike ride

For the end of the year it comes to *autumn*
Leaves start to turn brown, orange and red
And fall to the ground
People kicking them around, then children push them into a pile
Children start to look forward to Christmas
And writing their letters.

Lucy Boote (11)
Temple Guiting School

As ...

As happy as a child with a friend,
As happy as a duck on water.

As sad as a child with broken toys,
As sad as a daffodil with no water.

As lonely as a child with no friends,
As lonely as a ghost wandering the night.

As proud as a child winning a football match,
As proud as a geologist finding a new fossil.

As frightened as a child with a lion,
As frightened as a ship's captain on rough sea.

Patrick Carthew (11)
Temple Guiting School